Teen.

real teens

Diary of a Junior Year

volume 3

SCHOLASTIC INC.
New York Toronto London Auckland Sydney
Mexico City New Delhi Hong Kong

ISBN 0-439-08410-5

Distributed under license from
The Petersen Publishing Company, L.L.C.
Copyright © 1999 The Petersen Publishing
Company, L.L.C. All rights reserved.
Published by Scholastic Inc.

 Produced by 17th Street Productions,
a division of Daniel Weiss Associates, Inc.
33 West 17th Street, New York, NY 10011

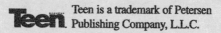 Teen is a trademark of Petersen
Publishing Company, L.L.C.

SCHOLASTIC and associated logos are trademarks and/or
registered trademarks of Scholastic Inc.

12 11 10 9 8 7 6 5 4 3 2 1   9/9 0 1 2 3 4/0

Printed in the U.S.A.   01
First Scholastic Printing, November 1999

Special Thanks to Laura Dower

Diary of a Junior Year

volume 3

The diaries you are about to read are real. Names, places, and other details have been changed to protect the teens involved. But what they have to say all really happened.

WhoWeAre WhoWeAre

Marybeth Miller:

I'm a wiseass. I can make just about anyone smile, even if they're feeling down in the dumps, and that's really important 2 me. Some days I consider myself fatter than others, but what are you gonna do, right? I run track and play basketball and keep on—so it's no big deal. Mostly I love just hanging out with my friends. Mom, Dad, and my brother and sister r cool 2, I guess. I mean, we don't <u>always</u> get along, but I pull thru. I don't think I would want anything else.

<u>LIKES:</u> My yellow Polo shirt
<u>DISLIKES:</u> People who can't take a joke

Billy Shim:

I'm an outgoing, crazy guy, but I have mixed feelings about it. I'm smart and get good grades, but I know that's not good enough so I need something that stands out like sports, sports, sports! The scene with my parents is totally up/down. We have great moments, but we have arguments too—like good grades = heaven and bad grades = hell. But my older brother Lee, who's playing football at college right now, he's always there for me. Lee is the nicest guy you could ever meet. I think things would be easier if I were more like him.

<u>LIKES:</u> Sports, sports, sports (esp. lacrosse in spring)

<u>DISLIKES:</u> Stupid, clingy chicks

<u>Teresa Falcone:</u>

There is much more going on in my mind than the eye can see . . . . I love writing, reading, dancing, singing, acting, playing field hockey, listening to all kinds of music, and most of all being with my friends and family. I know I'm smart and get really good grades, but I have this problem, which is everyone sees me as this airhead I hate that! Sometimes I can be sooooo insecure! My parents are divorced, so I live with my mom and my older brother Vincent, even though we don't get along ever My dad lives a town away, so I see him a lot

WhoWeAre WhoWeAre

<u>LIKES:</u> Romance books and anything else romantic!

<u>DISLIKES:</u> Not being taken seriously!

Jake Barosso:

Ladies think I'm cute, but only sometimes. I'm shy, but I love to dance and I'm always on the go. I love raving, riding a Jet Ski, playing pool, and fixing up my new car. My dad is really really sick, so things are terrible at home right now, but I try to help out as much as I can. We're always arguing about the stupidest things. I wish it didn't have to be like this. I like to make Mom + sis laugh whenever I can. I'm funny too.

<u>LIKES:</u> My car!!!

<u>DISLIKES:</u> Being sick + people who are assholes (a tie)

Katie Carson:

I am involved in Community Club and student council, on the tennis team, and a peer

4

ministry leader of my church, among other things. To fit it all into one word, I am well-rounded. My schedule is nuts, but I handle stress with my sense of humor. I have important long-term goals for myself. Sometimes my friends tell me I am naive about things, but I really do believe I have the ability to get along with <u>everyone</u>. The most important thing to me is family—we're very close and share a special bond. I can tell my mom everything.

<u>LIKES:</u> Musical theater, travel, good grades, Brad

<u>DISLIKES:</u> People who don't have any goals

<u>Edward</u> <u>Baxter</u>:

This is me. I'm all the characteristics associated with this picture. I love listening to music, watching TV, and playing Nintendo. I'm a yearbook editor, sometimes I run track and I'm in Community Club, even though I'm starting to hate it, and I mean REALLY HATE IT. I'm also a bad speller, but for the most part I do well in school. As far as parents go, mine

are like big kids. My dad is a real comedian and my mom is
stupid funny, like me. My older brother Jerry is away at college.
LIKES: Coconut my dog
DISLIKES: People who never call you back, especially
when you beep them

Emma West:

I think I'm totally trustworthy, kind,
and respectful, but if someone starts
talking about me behind my back I feel a
lot different and I get upset. At school
I'm ice-hockey manager and I'm in
Community Club and student council. I
love hanging out but I usually don't make
any plans until like the last minute,
usually with marybeth. The most important
thing is that my friends mean the world
to me. my parents are cool too. They're
always running around doing a million
different things and my little brother
Ronnie thinks he runs the house. my
sister Lynn and I have to babysit for him

a lot, which can be a drag but whatever.
  <u>LIKES:</u> Having a boyfriend
  <u>DISLIKES:</u> Being left out

<u>Kevin Moran.</u>
  I'm All this: smart, funny, hyper,
And I don't know what else kind of
guy. I kinda go from one thing to
Another like wave running, clubbing,
swimming, mainly Any sport—And mostly
just chilling with my friends. Still,
I get bored All the time. My
family, they're loud, And Dad has
been married 2x so we have A lotta
freakin people here to deal with
And we Argue like ALL THE TIME
but thAt's cool I guess cuz I
reAlly do love them All. I wAs
reAlly close to my sis LenA, but she
died like 8 yeARS Ago when I wAs 8,
which still mAkes me mAd.
  <u>LIKES:</u> DRessing And doing stuff
exActly AS I wAnt it And no one
cAn tell me Anything else
  <u>DISLIKES:</u> My bRotheR Neil no
doubt!

7

Jake

December 12

Why do I have the worst life? I mean, today I had fun hanging out with my friends and I bought two CDs, which was cool, like I was feeling the Christmas spirit and all that. Then the bad part happened. When I came home, my dad asked to talk to me—and of course all this stuff was like rushing into my head. He said he had some bad news and I thought he was gonna say something about himself but then he said one of my cousins, Frankie, died. He was hit by a car.

Why Frankie? He was only 21. I was pissed. Why am I losing all the people that mean something to me? Frankie never did anything wrong. I cried tonight for so long I thought I wouldn't stop. I used to hang out w/Frankie when we were kids. I was thinking about how we would spend time at his house and play baseball because that is what he loved best. And now he's gone.

Katie

December 12
@ 11 A.M.

Where has the time gone? A lot of really big stuff is coming up in the next week:

1.   HUGE concert for choir plus lots of others in next month

2.   Tryouts for the musical on Wed. I am really nervous!

3.   Get my paperwork together for the National Community Club Adviser Board—elections are in a couple of weeks and I could get picked to represent our area!

4.   My family's Christmas holiday party (this year my mom is asking almost 200 people!)

5.   Deadline for the Intrastate Committee

My first priority though has to be *SLEEP.* I have to keep an eye on my schedule because the truth is that the time of year when I am most likely to burn out is around Jan/Feb, when the musical starts. It is so exhausting! Music and acting are my new passions! It started last year when my relationship with Robert crashed. That was when I first auditioned for the school play, *The Women.* At first, that was just a distraction, but really it turned into so much more.

When I first auditioned, all I could hope for was a small, walk-on part, but then I was cast as the *lead!* That did so much for my confidence. Acting is a talent I never expected to be gifted with, but luckily I am. This year the musical is *The Boy Friend* and tryouts always make me so nervous. But *I MUST BELIEVE IN MYSELF* if I have any hopes of being cast. I'd love to play the part of Polly because she is the lead and she's a soprano (like me), but I would be happy with one of the other girl characters like Fay or Nancy I guess. They'll probably cast me as Polly though because I look like her, and I would have to learn how to dance the Charleston because all the girls in the play are flapper girls! I *REALLY* want a lead! That would be the best Christmas gift.

Baxter

December 12

Tonight my mom put up the Christmas tree and that has really put me in the spirit of the holidays. We put on Christmas music and we all started dancing around. I love my parents so much. They're good people.

I didn't mention that yesterday I had a terrible experience at school. I was standing in the hall and I saw Megan. It wasn't like usual, she was alone, and so I went over to her and started talking. Of course something had to ruin it because then Marybeth and Emma both came over and poked me in the back. They were saying, "Hi Bax," in this really stupid voice. I could have killed them. Everyone always does that to me. I know they mean it as fun. But it isn't always that fun. Anyway, maybe I'll say something to Emma tonight. Maybe I won't.

Marybeth

December 12th

Tonight Matt and me went out, which was so great. Okay, here's what happened. When we were talking online this afternoon I asked him if he wanted to hang out w/me and first he said he didn't think it was a good idea (bummer) but THEN suddenly out of nowhere he changed his mind and was like, "Do you wanna go to the driving range?" So we did! Later on we were at his house and watched *Good Will Hunting,* which was kinda boring so then he played his guitar 4 a little bit. I had fun. I dunno if he did. One time right before he took me home he seemed bored. He even said, "I'm kinda bored." I wonder what that meant. Was it me? Will he say n e thing to n e one? He seems so shy sometimes.

Anyway, later on I talked to one of his best pals Lance who is actually a pretty good friend of mine too. I wanted the real story! Lance said something about how he can tell that Matt likes me b/c he *doesn't* talk about me. I was like WHAT?! That doesn't make any sense to me. But Lance says that's just how Matt is. He doesn't open up about good stuff. If Matt *didn't* like me he would probably already have talked. Whatever that logic means. I sorta don't believe him.

The weird thing about talking to Lance though was finding out that he doesn't even really think Matt is a very nice person, which totally confused me.

11

Lance says Matt makes fun of him a lot, calling him a dumb jerk and stuff, and hearing that really bothered me. Why would Lance make up shit like that unless it were true?

Whether I get together with Matt or not, I realize I am lucky 2 have so many good peeps in my life like Lance. When we were done talking he told me that the guy who snags me will be lucky. That was sweet. He made me feel good.

Kevin

12/13

Well, today I feel really crappy. I can't really go out b/c my throat is sore so I watched *Titanic* tonight and that was cool for like a minute until I started feeling all hot and fevery. I told Adina she shouldn't even bother coming over. I dunno for some reason I just wasn't into seeing her, feeling like this. We've been going out for 3 months and now it's like different all of a sudden. Hopefully she won't get all freaky on me. I hate it so much when winter starts and you wanna be all into the holiday spirit and shit and then you just get ILL. I am sick of being sick. Ta ta, peace out!

Emma

Cliff hasn't called me yet. We're supposed to hang out. I really hope he's feeling okay. He hurt his hand because he fell skating the other day and this morning when we talked he said it hurt. I worry about him a lot—I can't help myself. He went skating today and said he would get home and call me as soon as he did, at the latest 8:30. Now it's 7:58 and he hasn't called.

Today was a nice day since I hung out with Marybeth and her mom at the mall. I really wanted to get my dad a Christmas gift but I didn't know what to get. I can't buy him shirts or pants because I don't know what size he wears. Actually, my mom told me not to worry about Dad because she would just buy him stuff and put me and my brother & sister's names on it. Normally me and my sister Lynn don't get our parents anything. They tell us not to get them anything and so we don't. And me and my sister don't exchange gifts either which is ok with both of us. I wonder what I will get this year. I haven't asked for anything really good. Oh well.

13

Marybeth

December 13th

Today I went shopping w/my mom and Emma and I bought the majority of my Xmas gifts. Mom gets a sweater and Dad gets socks. It's kind of funny now that I think about it b/c I bought the stuff w/babysitting money but all of my friends' parents usually give them $ to buy gifts, so basically they end up paying for their own gifts. But not me. Not in my neck o' the woods.

I'm usually way more into Xmas. But for some reason it just seems like I have so much on my mind. I wonder why that is? I wonder what's gonna happen w/me and Matt? I wonder if things are gonna be new & different next year? I can't stop thinking.

Billy

12-13

I can't believe it's already the middle of December and that Xmas is only 12 days away. I have this weird awareness of time lately. But thankfully I have more of it. Like it is only 10 at night when I am writing this and that's pretty early for me to be done with homework. The reason that's true is because tonight I started studying at 6 instead of 8 like I used to when

14

we had football. Oh yeah. *FOOTBALL IS REALLY OVER!* What a nuisance it turned into. I have so much more time now and I am home by 4 at least, which is great.

Something that isn't so great though is that I got a speeding ticket. I was going 46 in a 25 zone or at least that's what the cop said. I think I might go fight the ticket rather than get stuck with a shitty fine. My court date is sometime in a couple of weeks. Of course I got yelled at and now my parents don't trust me. I swear they are ready to do anything to make me miserable. Like I can't drive now as punishment. I can't believe they won't even consider bargaining with me to pick something else that I can't do. Why does it have to be driving?

Teresa

Dec 13 (12:30 pm)

Dear Diary,

I can't do anything right. I've decided this. Ever since my Sweet 16 I feel so introspective, and one of the things I have been thinking of more than other things is my innate ability to mess things up. I mean, I know that some of the kids at school think I am this total bubblehead and sure, I mess stuff up. But it's like never ending.

Like with Leonardo, the really cute Italian guy I was checking out at the hockey game the other day.

Did I *really* think that one was going anywhere? Of course it hasn't and obviously I must have done something to mess it up, right? I mean, I haven't even had a real conversation with him yet, right?

And today it was shopping. Usually I am so good at buying things, but I have been trying to figure out what in the world I could possibly get Gina and Wendy and Stephanie and Marybeth and Sherelle and . . . *EVERYONE* for Christmas. I just have way too many people to shop for! Plus it's like I am blocked—if I can't buy for one of them, I can't buy for any of them. What am I going to do?

Mom says I shouldn't worry. I'm a pretty girl and a smart girl and I will figure it all out. She says I should just have a good time and not obsess.

Kevin

12/14

Now to start off with I know that my parents are great don't get me wrong I couldn't really ask for anything more in my life b/c they give me whatever I need and all that. And I don't want to sound too spoiled *BUT*—and there is always a but—they really piss me off, I mean *PISS ME OFF*. They just don't understand me. I mean of course I know sometimes I can be wrong but a lot of times I get frustrated b/c I know I'm right. I am constantly doubted. Ok, so this is what is going on. I came home and my mom had gotten a letter in the mail from school and she forgot to tell me about it. She just *FORGOT*. And she said it was no big deal but it was a big deal, ok? Ok, maybe I am just still feeling sick and so I'm more mad than I usually get but it doesn't matter b/c the point is that she and I got into it and my dad was just like sitting there not doing anything. I hate that more than anything b/c it's like he's not listening or paying attention and that is always what he does w/me and my brother Neil too. He just pretends like Neil isn't so full of it and Dad just keeps putting up w/his crap. I mean HE is the one who is like the total mess right now and instead of getting into trouble, he just gets away w/it all. I am somehow mysteriously like out of nowhere the one that my parents distrust. I am suddenly the one and they are like *TOTALLY* denying it also. They won't admit that, but they are. That's all there really is to it. Ta ta

p.s. Of course in the middle of the whole argument my mom brought up my not going to church and I was kinda like why is my mother such a pain, like is that her *JOB*? Ta ta

Teresa

Dec 14 (9:50 pm)

Dear Diary,

It's Monday and I had a boring day. Even my horoscope today was depressing.

17

LIBRA: Social Life 'n' Love: A romantic situation will develop—but not yet. Watch your back. Someone has his eyes on you, but you may be blinded by his x-ray stare. He knows your deepest secrets before you tell him. Beware: He's out to steal your heart. Take it slow.

I think I need to tone down on my love vibes and just deal w/my homework for a while. I did write this short essay for English class about Mom. I think it's ok. It's pretty much what I worked on over the weekend (since I was fairly dateless).

My mom loved it but of course she would—LOL. Actually, she cried. We've gotten so close lately, like she can read my mind.

MOTHER
by Teresa J. Falcone

My first birthday is when it all started. That is when my mother made me in all ways great and small. She is a magical person who gave me life, not only literally, but symbolically.

My mother is the leading person responsible for my development. She has used her love for people, her support, and her character to build me up to be the person I am today. Calling my mother a significant life force would be an understatement. Without her, there is no me. Without me, she says she is also lost.

Being with my mother brings a smile to my face. I am blessed in more ways than one. Not only does she support me financially and love me, but I also consider her a best friend. Anytime I need someone to talk to she is here for me unconditionally. She plays different roles in my life too. First, she is the mother who sticks up for me and my brother Vincent. Next, she stands by me no matter what. Finally, she is my confidante and friend. Her tender loving care gets me through rough times. She is always there, as a tree is in rain or snow. I can truly count on my mother.

Life sometimes feels like it can get the best of me, but when that happens, I let go. I have someone to care for me and somewhere to turn to. No matter what else is going on in my life, she is all I need to go on. She touches me like an angel. She is my support and my role model.

Who Our Role Models Are

Kevin:

Jake is definitely the coolest b/c he knows how to control his feelings. I don't think I have any famous role models, but I know I wanna be one. It would feel good to know that despite what I think of my weird life, everything I am doing and everything I am feeling looks right in someone else's eyes.

Jake:

Other than Kevin, there really is no friend I look up to, and anyone famous that I admire is because they worked hard and made it to the top. Sometimes I think it's me who is a role model because a lot of the kids in the middle school look up to me.

Emma:

I really dunno. I admire my cousin Barb. She really applies herself and knows how to be happy.

Who Our Role Models Are

Billy:
   My older brother Lee.

Teresa:
   I look up to my mom of course and my neighbor Stephanie because she is nurturing and NEVER jealous and I wish I could be like that. As far as anyone major, that's Baxter. His attitude is the best of anyone I have ever known. The kid is ALWAYS smiling.

Katie:
   All my role models at school have graduated. My parents are my only real role models I do admire my friends for different reasons but really it's as if roles are reversed now b/c the younger kids look up to me just like I looked up to older students when I was a frosh/sophomore. Of course, I am honored to be able to guide them in the way I was guided.

Who Our Role Models Are

<u>Baxter:</u>

I look up to my pal Derek because of his easygoing attitude about life but I also look up to Marybeth because of her complete outgoingness.

<u>Marybeth:</u>

As far as famous role models, I look up to Jewel. I would give anything to be a good writer and singer like her or Sarah McLachlan. And I really value Kevin's opinion on stuff.

Katie

Brad has been so good to me lately—I love him! He is so supportive. Not like Robert, who was *always* so jealous and competitive with me in all areas like drama and music.

Brad knows exactly what to say to make me melt. He's the last person I talk to before I go to sleep and the first person I talk to when I wake up.

Yesterday we hung out with his older brother Karl and his girlfriend Cindy—and I found out that Karl has gone almost four months without seeing her. I can't imagine that! I have extensive trouble just going for three days without seeing Brad! When we were together Cindy promised that she'd teach me how to ski. She skis all the time in Switzerland, where she's from. I'm such a klutz so who knows if I can keep up, but she wants to try. The four of us have such a good time together.

I think the best part about my whole relationship with Brad is the fact that I don't feel dependent on him. I am not known as "Brad's girlfriend," I am always known as Katie, always my own person. I think the fact that we **don't** see each other *every single day* means we have a **healthier** relationship than some other people I know. I miss him when we're apart, but it's better that way for the long term.

23

Jake

December 15

I didn't see my cousin Frankie enough before he died. I wish I had spent more time with him. I have been thinking about how I was planning to go see him when the weather was a little better, but I couldn't get off work. I did not think his day would come so soon. He and I are so close in age. And now it's too late. Too late for a visit, and too late for goodbyes. I wish I could talk to someone about all this. Tomorrow night is Frankie's wake and then they'll have the funeral. I can't stop thinking. Did I do something wrong to make all this happen?

Emma

12/15, 11:23 PM

I am so lucky to have a friend like Betsy Geffen. She is always there for me. Whenever I am in trouble, she knows what to say exactly to make me feel better. We don't spend as much time together as we used to but we are definitely still tight. Some people say we look like twins actually and Cliff even got us mixed up once, which was so weird. Anyway, it's not like I am feeling totally sad or anything today, but she knew I did badly on one test and I haven't heard from Cliff

24

for the whole day so I'm a little upset. So Betsy sent me this poem on e-mail that she got from somewhere or made up. I don't know which.

> When you are lost
> I know how to find you
> When you are worried
> I will give you a light
> To shine the way and make
> You feel comforted
> When you are alone
> And want someone to listen
> Reach out for me
> I am always there
> I am ready
> To laugh and cry and sing
> To dance and jump and smile
> I will be your friend,
> Always your friend.

I can't write poems on my own, but I know a good one when I see one, and I really like this one.

I hope Cliff calls soon.

marybeth

December 15th

This morning in gym class Sherelle was singing "You've Lost That Loving Feeling" and guess what's been stuck in my head all day long? That song! Tonight I am feeling so tired. It's like 8:30 but I can't go to sleep yet.

I got the best news ever earlier online. One of Matt's best friends, this girl Mara, has started to become friends w/me lately and she is really really really nice. How cool is that!? She's trying to find out for me what Matt is thinking b/c according to her he hardly ever talks about girls but suddenly he talks about *ME* all the time. Mara says she can keep me informed and tell me what's up. That is such good news! It made my night. Wow. I am really falling for *MATT*. It sux! Oh well, maybe I will go to bed after all. Good nite!!

Kevin

12/15

Today is Tuesday and we started up this volleyball thing in gym and it really kicked ass! Me + 3 friends we play the best of everyone and call each other the Hot Squad. It's me + Micky Lazlo + 2 other girls, my BFFs Pam, who has the nicest chest but I wouldn't ever tell her that, and Cristina, the one I wanted to take the swing class with when Adina got all jealous and shit. I would say playing volleyball w/them is the best thing these days b/c we laugh the whole time. Other than that not much is happening except life guarding, which I had yesterday. That life-guarding instructor is pretty dope—I wouldn't mind getting together w/her! Truth is that I still feel kinda sick though so even though I went into the pool yesterday I decided to blow off our swim meet against Joyce today. Anyway, that's it. School is like the most boring thing going. I hate it so much. All I do is homework and more homework. Well, I'm gonna chill and watch Buffy slay some vampires now. Maybe I'll call Adina.

Katie

December 16
@ 1:36 P.M.
Classes like chemistry and math are slowly improving, so I am feeling pretty good about school right now. I do have some butterflies in my stomach though since tryouts for the musical are later today. I am questioning my acting and singing abilities, which is not a good thing. Am I really good enough to get a lead?

Later @ 6:30 P.M.
It doesn't happen too often that I am this much of a nervous wreck but today that was certainly true. I

was really doubting if I had any talent at all. I honestly did not think I was going to be okay for try-outs—I just couldn't pull myself together. I NEVER get like that, I usually have nerves of steel. What was happening to me? Well, lucky for me I was walking down the hall at JFK right before the tryout and I saw Jaclyn Roome! She was back from college and just visiting our old music teacher *JUST AS I WAS ABOUT TO GO IN AND PRACTICE!* She saw me and immediately knew something was up and that I needed some support. She said that I had nothing to worry about and that I was one of the most talented kids at JFK. It was like she knew how to bring me the confidence I needed at just the right time. It made me realize how much I missed having her and other friends from her class around. I liked so much being "the baby" last year, always feeling like someone older and smarter was there to help out.

So then it was 7th period and I went into the bathroom to brush my hair and put on some makeup. At least I looked good. That strengthened my confidence. When I walked into the audition though my stomach did a *TOTAL* flip-flop because there were 65 girls there and only 7 or so female parts in *The Boy Friend!* And only like 3 leads! Nevertheless I got up there (after everyone else had gone) and I sang okay but I acted the best, better than I ever have. Jaclyn came to watch & said I blew everyone away. Afterward I went home for a tutoring session, which took 2 long hours, and then I got the *BIGGEST*

SURPRISE. Mom and Dad bought me 2 tickets last minute to go to the Starlight Christmas Concert in the city. It's a bunch of bands and stuff and I am going tomorrow! My mom said that I should bring Brad with me. I am so glad that auditions are *over* and now I can go to the concert. Hooray!

Billy

12-16

I really wish I had never hooked up with Blair D. She is still trying to talk to me in the halls and we have been over for weeks now. What am I supposed to do without sounding like a total asshole? I just want her to go away. I don't want to be her friend anymore. I don't know what my problem is because I mostly just hook up with girls and then I don't want to make it into any kind of long-term relationship. I just don't know how to evolve it into love or anything. I find a lot of girls who like me but I don't know how to handle it really beyond just talking or hooking up. Maybe I should ask Lee what he thinks. He always knows how to act in these situations. L8er for love . . .

Teresa

Dec 16 (7:25 p.m.)

Dear Diary,

I thought it was later than Wednesday! Oh my gosh, this week is going sooooo slowly! But only 9 more days until Christmas. Hooray! Mom & I put up the tree and it looks *AWESOME*. I can't believe that it's the end of another year. I am already thinking of New Year's resolutions and the #1 priority has to be to get up off my butt and start doing what I want to do! I am so sick of sitting back and watching life whiz past me I have to do something about it!!!

I need to go even deeper inside of myself and discover who I really am because right now I know I am at a tough age. I don't really know who I am, where I am going, or what I want to do, and it's kinda scary but I have to start talking about it more.

Today at school I got my essay back on mothers and my teacher gave me a B+ because she said I could have been more specific but otherwise she really liked it. I am going to work more on my writing to make it even better! That would be sooooo cool to get published for writing a story like I did for writing a poem. I must ♥ my work!

Don't forget to get presents for
Mom & Dad!

Baxter

December 16

Tonight I studied for 4 hours for tomorrow's chem test. Yesterday Mr. MacTaggart gave us four sheets of paper with 17 molecules and 15 things for each—so I had to memorize over 200 different things with only one day to do it.

Community Club is getting worse. Miss Shapiro never lets up on me! What a total bitch. I wish I didn't have to listen to her. She actually wrote me up on a slip saying that my contributions to the group had been slipping. Now my parents have to sign it. How weird and unfair. I am seriously thinking of giving up on CC because I think she has it in for me. Of course the irony is that today I was elected into the National Honor Society. I am really happy about that.

Emma

12/16, 8:36 PM

I am feeling pretty happy right now. I'm watching *Dawson's Creek* and things are good with Cliff *now*. Last night was bad though. We got into this big fight. He got really mad because I invited him to come with me and my family on Sunday before Christmas comes. There's this special party at my aunt's house every year and one of the local police captains who is a friend of hers dresses up as Santa and everything. Anyway, we started fighting because Cliff kept telling me that he has already done the "family thing," and he doesn't want to do it again. I realized when he said that he had done it already that he was talking about when he was with his ex-girlfriend Rebecca. That is totally not fair as far as I am concerned. That was what got me really upset. It hurt my feelings because I am *NOT* Rebecca and anyway just because he did it once doesn't mean he did it with *ME*, which is what matters. He has to do it with me.

We did make up finally. He said he would go. We were on the telephone actually and my mom yelled from across the room to him, "See you Sunday! We have a present for you, Cliff!" He heard that and now he knows he has to show up. I started laughing because he was kind of embarrassed about having gotten mad and everything. Now he says he's excited to come. I can't wait to show him the present too. It's bright red boxers with Taz on the butt. They are soooo cute I know he will love them.

The funniest thing was that right before we said goodbye he was like, "Do I have to sit on Santa's lap?" I told him to wait and see. Of course he has to do it whether he wants to or not! And I wanna get a picture of him doing it too! It's so fun to have someone I am dating at Christmastime because he keeps asking me what I want and I can't wait to get something from him that he picks out himself.

Oh well, *Dawson's Creek* just ended. I better go study for chemistry.

Jake

December 16

Everyone is getting so into that stupid concert tomorrow and it pisses me off. It just seems so insignificant compared to everything and everyone else. Why did Frankie have to die? I am so sad it's like I'm heavy with sadness. I want to talk to Frankie again so much but he's not alive. I know that he is probably in a better place now but if I could bring him back and give him a longer life I would do it.

Tonight I got two leads from work and that is good. I should get a good commission from them if they work out. The thing is that tonight in particular work was a good way to take my mind off things for a little while but on the way home I couldn't help but think about how my dad is getting sicker and one day it will be his turn to go. I am soooo worried about that time for him. I know my father has been a lucky man in life and that he has a good family and a house and all that, but it is still way too soon for him to be going anywhere but here. It's just not fair for anyone to have to leave so soon.

Baxter

December 17

Life may suck sometimes, but if you hang in there, you get rewarded. My four hours of studying *TOTALLY* paid off because I think I did *VERY* well on that chemistry test from hell. Everyone else was bummed out but not me. Tomorrow I have a physics test. It never stops, but now I am doing well so I don't mind it as much.

As far as Megan goes, we flirt constantly. Something is *DEFINITELY* going on.

Kevin

12/17

I am *SO WIRED*! This day has been speeding by so quick I don't believe it! Sixth period really sucked today b/c we had to take some freakin tests in an SAT review. It was bad and real boring. I'm not sure how much longer I can take it but at least it went quickly. I am feeling so much better the cold is *GONE*. My swim coach said that if we wanna race on the team we have to get up on Thursday mornings before the Friday races and practice before school even starts and so that's what we were doing this morning. I wonder if maybe that's why I am so *WIRED*. Waking up at 6 for a 6:15 practice was *REAL, REAL* hard. But

I did it fortunately. Plus we don't have to book it to class until 2nd period when we have morning swim so that was good. Me and Micky Lazlo also didn't have to take gym. It was ok too b/c for once in school I was actually *AWAKE*. Usually I'm such a load these days. Maybe I have that thing where you get depressed when you don't have enuf sunlight—what's it called?

I thought maybe I would go to the Starlight Christmas Concert tonite but since I am writing this right now at like 10 at night obviously I did not go. Adina's dad knows someone who could've gotten us tickets but he couldn't pull thru it was too late I guess. Lazlo and his girl, Katie, and Marybeth are just a couple of the people who are there I know so I bet they're having a blast. But it feels good to have a little time on my hands tonite. I haven't had that in a while. Ok, I gotta go study for math. Peace out!

Marybeth

December 17th

It is so late but I can't sleep. The Starlight Christmas Concert was rocking and I am still pretty wired from all the music. I am so glad I went! Thank God my cousins got me a ticket. They were a little quiet when we got there, but of course I am far from shy! I have NO PROBLEM dancing by myself and I did. The Goo Goo Dolls were the best!

Maybe it would've been more fun w/Matt there. But he is such a playa! That is not looking good. The last couple of days have been kind of depressing and so I needed something to cheer me up.

Yesterday was the worst. I got up my nerve to call Matt and we were talking on the phone and he was like making fun of me and stuff, which was really funny and cool and then all of a sudden he stopped. He said he had to get off and could he just call me back. I mean, I risked calling him and he hung up on me. And then I didn't think he would call back and he didn't or at least he hasn't since, and that really hurts my self-esteem. So then I e-mailed his friend Mara to ask her what she thought and she said that I should just chill out b/c Matt has an attitude problem sometimes even w/people that he loves. She said that there are "plenty of fish in da sea, but that I should hang in there if he's the one I want."

Should I start looking for a new man? What a bummer. I really liked Matt. I thought this was gonna be special somehow but I dunno if I can handle his head games. Anyway, I will not call him anymore. Not after what he did. I will wait for HIM TO CALL ME—absolutely!

I wonder if guys realize how dumb they are sometimes. They are so stupid always thinking they r the shit when they are really ALL dorks.

Teresa

Dec 18 (5:45 p.m.)

Dear Diary,

I was at the hockey game tonite and Leonardo was there too. But he didn't even wave. He usually does. Why are guys so thick sometimes? I was so hoping that he would come over and talk to me sometime. Wrong! I am clueless, as usual.

Anyway, I went to two JFK hockey games as I said and there usually aren't that many people at the games but for some weird reason tonite there were *SOOOOOOOO* many people. I walked in the place and that's the worst when there are huge crowds because everyone stares at you. And I know they were all talking about me. Well, we ended up winning so there was an upside to the whole night.

I have been working on a poem about music because I listen to it so much. I think it's important to write about stuff that's important in my life. I can really lose myself in music and words. Maybe I should write a poem about hockey too—ha ha!

Jake

December 18

Frankie's brother wrote such a good eulogy for him and it touched my heart so much. Oh yeah, I took off from school today to go to Frankie's funeral. There were so many people there, family and friends. The one thing I really hate about listening to everyone though is how they always use the words *gift* and *celebration*. I am sorry, but someone dying is NOT a gift and it is NOT a time to celebrate. Yes, Frankie is going on to a better place and all that but it is not a celebration that he's leaving us.

My mom and I were crying a lot. She is upset like me and she keeps saying how unfair it is that this has to happen to someone as good as Frankie or my father too. I can't stand this anymore. All I want to do is live life to the fullest as if it were my last day and time to go tomorrow. I don't want to spend all my time feeling bad. I want to feel good for a change.

What Makes Me Feel Good

<u>Teresa</u>:
   There are sooooo many great feelings! Last summer me & Sherelle said that it felt pretty good to be checked out by a guy even though he was already with another girl! Of course we were just kidding around, but it does feel good to get checked out.

<u>Baxter</u>:
   It feels so good when someone sends you a card or calls you up just to tell you they were thinking of you.

<u>Katie</u>:
   Being in Brad's arms.

<u>Billy</u>:
   Joking around makes me feel good. I like it when someone can make me laugh. Life is too serious all the time.

What Makes Me Feel Good

<u>Jake</u>:
Feeling loved.

<u>Emma</u>:
The best feeling in the whole world is not just having someone who loves you in your life, but having them tell you all the time that they do.

<u>Kevin</u>:
I'd say sex is the best feeling but I don't know what that's like. So then the next best thing is speeding along and knowing I am in control but being on the edge of being out of control.

<u>Marybeth</u>:
When you get to the top of a roller coaster + go plunging down + you get that "airy" feeling in your tummy.

Kevin

I thought things w/me and Adina were going good but now I think maybe something is up. Here's the deal, when I'm w/Adina I'm psyched but when she isn't around I *don't* know, I feel like I *don't* miss her a lot and stuff like that. It's weird. It's like I can't make up my mind what I feel. I've been thinking maybe I'm crushing on someone else, my friend Cristina. It's like I have soooo much in common w/her and I'm never bored around her and there's always something to say. I enjoy times w/Cristina but I *don't* want to ruin the friendship we have by making more of it. With Adina, it's just that we *don't* have that much in common and she doesn't really talk a lot. I do all the talking. *I WISH I COULD FIGURE EVERYTHING OUT W/MY LOVE LIFE!* When I think I know what I want, I realize that I *don't* want it. I honestly wonder how long me and Adina are gonna last. I can't say. I *don't* wanna hurt her and I *DO* care but obviously things just aren't working anymore. I obviously have changed if I am having feelings for this *other* person.

STOP THINKING ABOUT IT NOW. Okay, that didn't work ha ha.

Anyway, one more thing that was funny today was when Lazlo was in math class he was wearing shades b/c he was so dog tired from that Starlight Christmas shindig last nite in the city. He looked pretty phat but the teachers were like, "Take off the glasses, Mickey." Ha! Ha! Anyway, later on he was *HURTING* in a major way at the swim meet. How do you get a walking zombie to compete in a swim race? The coach was PO'ed. Lazlo bailed on the race and so we lost b/c he is one of the best swimmers. Coach was happy w/my performance though. I am more determined than ever to swim the 100 yd. freestyle and break the record, since I am only like 4 seconds off. Only 4 seconds! Breaking a record would be the coolest thing ever.

Emma

12/18, 4:48 PM

Get this! Katie went to the Starlight Christmas Concert with her boyfriend Brad! I didn't know she went! This sucks! Major, major gossip.

So here's why it's not cool *AT ALL*. Someone told me this and it's a little messed up because the last time I talked to Katie about it she said her mom couldn't get any tickets for any of us, *including her*. For the past two years a whole group of us have gone together, but this year when all our parents tried to get tickets, no one could get through, except Katie, who said she had gotten us tickets. Okay, then we were all really psyched! But a few days later she said she didn't have them anymore all of a sudden and we

42

all thought that was a little weird, but whatever. Truthfully, the person who was most upset by it was Sherelle because Katie was like her only chance at getting tickets. Marybeth got hers at the last minute through one of her cousins. I don't know. I don't want to make a big deal out of it, but I think Sherelle might say something. Like I am over it. I don't care that I didn't go because I went 2x already and the more important thing is that my sister Lynn went (her friend got her a ticket and she wanted really badly to see 'N SYNC). So she told me all about it. But Sherelle is another story. Whatever.

p.s. Today I have my period and it is just so uncomfortable. Oh well, the only good thing is that now I won't have it on Christmas day.

Katie

December 18
@ 5:15 P.M.

I love being busy at Christmastime! Yesterday was so jam-packed. From choir to the *AMAZING* Starlight Concert, I feel like I am ready for anything!

First, we had an all-day field trip with the choir. We went to different schools around town. Then we did a special choir performance at the Senior Center, where I actually volunteer sometimes. My choir director said that I have a special way with the people there. I am glad he notices stuff like that in me. I feel so good after performing for them.

The last thing I did was go with Brad to the Starlight Christmas Concert! Hooray! We just barely made the train at 7:08 and ended up getting there more than a half hour late, but Brad was okay with that. It reminded me of going *last* year with Robert. Back then, I bought the tickets and paid for parking and everything and all he could do was complain because we were five minutes late. Five minutes! Brad is so much nicer than Robert ever was. Brad never lets me pay for ANYTHING (which can sometimes be annoying but we never fight).

The only bad part about today was something I heard through the grapevine. Apparently Sherelle was really mad about the fact that I took Brad to the concert instead of her. She thinks I'm breaking some tradition by not doing it. I know that last year I was the one who got her ticket, but things are just different now. She has no right to expect that from me. Ever since school started she has been totally caught up in her relationship with Bobby and so has Marybeth and neither of them really call me anymore. Why should I go out of my way to please them?

Marybeth

December 18th

Right now I am hysterically crying. I just had a huge blowup with my brother, who has been *on my back* all day long and we just finished dinner and I went to go online and I saw that the computer was plugged into his line. I asked really nicely if I could go on real quick and he didn't even answer a yes or a no. So I said, "Why do you have to be such a dick about it?!" and of course he ignored me. So I said it again and then I said that if he *wasn't* such a dick that I wouldn't hate him so much.

This morning was even worse when I asked (really nicely, I might add) if I could borrow a CD. Just one lousy CD! And he said to me in that stupid tone of voice that he gets when he is acting all superior and older than me, "I don't think so," and a bunch of other stuff I can't repeat. I was like, Mitch you are such a jerk *ALL THE TIME*, why is that? And I slammed my bedroom door.

I am not talking to him until he apologizes and I mean that.

Now it's later and I am
a little more calm I think
@ 11:20 P.M.

I am soooo tired and mad from the fight w/Mitch and from babysitting earlier today and it just seems

45

like *there is so much to do and so little time to do it!* Oh yeah, I almost forgot the weirdest thing of all that happened to me and Em today. I was talking to Emma and we have noticed this major change in Sherelle lately like she can't be bothered w/us or hang out w/us. Today we only talked for like 1 minute and then she said she had to take a shower. Huh? I prob. won't talk to her now until Monday in school. No joke. I can't believe that we aren't even talking about hanging out on Saturday like we always used to. Funny how things change so fast, right? Today was a really depressing day as far as relationships go.

Billy

12-19

I am so glad that Saturday is finally here! I love it! This week has been boring, just tests, homework, and the usual.

The only new thing is that this week we had a lot of holiday singing. But our trip the other day to some schools and the Senior Center was pretty cool, I have to admit that. It's cool because we learn all these different songs like Jewish songs for Hanukkah and then traditional Christmas carols and then some snow songs for people who just aren't that into religion I guess.

The best part of the singing field trip was def. *MISSING CLASSES*! Plus when we were visiting the other schools, I saw some pretty cute-looking 8th graders. Well, I guess maybe they're a little young even for me. Heh heh!!!

Last nite I went out to eat w/some other friends and went to a party at Katie's house and sang karaoke, which was fun. I really like to sing—I am realizing that more and more and more. It was great that her dad got one of those karaoke machines. I did like 2 songs. Bax and Kevin were there too and we sang "Frosty the Snowman" as a joke.

Baxter

December 19

CLAP THIS!!

BAXTER IS THE BOMB!!

WE ARE THE BEST SINGERS!!

MERRY CHRISTMAS AND HAPPY NEW YEAR!!

E. B. ♥ M. R.

I made these stickers at Katie's Christmas party on Friday night. It was so much fun. And I finally got to drive in Kevin's car. He is so lucky.

47

Tonight we celebrated Christmas Eve dinner. It's earlier than the real Christmas Eve because some other members of my family are leaving Monday for a vacation to this resort in North Carolina. But we wanted to still be able to celebrate together. My brother is home from college too.

My mom made twice-baked potatoes that I *LOVE* and I got some presents early, like an electric razor and a gift certificate to Old Navy from my gramps. Now I can get some more clothes for school. This is turning out to be a great week.

Jake

December 19

This month is not so good. I am just not having a good time. I haven't started my shopping and I have no clue about what to get my family. Frankie died and my dad is sick still and nothing is going my way. Last night I went to this girl Camille's Sweet 16 party. Jonny and I DJ'ed it. But it wasn't too good because it was too small and no girls who dance went. I couldn't dance with anyone.

The only good thing going on is that this weekend I hooked up with that girl Diana Russo that I've been talking to since the other day. I think she is really interested in me. She is good-looking and has a great body but she is only 14 so I guess maybe it won't work out. We'll see. I am still kind of hooked on Claudia.

p.s. Katie's party was last night too but I decided not to go. I just don't feel right.

Katie

December 19
@ 11 P.M.

I can't believe this! Yesterday I found out that I had a callback for the musical *The Boy Friend*. Out of 65 girls who auditioned, only 8 of us got callbacks! But the thing is that my competitor for the lead is *RACHEL ROSS*! I can't believe it! Somehow we always end up against each other. I am going to practice all weekend to beat her. I have to. First the yearbook, then tennis, and now *this*?

Yesterday night was my family's Christmas party here at our house and we had a great time, as always. It was catered and this karaoke guy came too. Everyone was talking and singing and having a good time. My mom told me that 5 or 6 of the adults at the party told her how impressed they were with Brad, that he was so handsome and well mannered. He passed the inspection! My aunt said he was as cute as a button. How corny! My family sure knows how to embarrass me.

So many friends came to the party and that was really nice, like Gwen, Billy, Baxter, Kevin, and of course Brad as I said. I guess there was a Sweet 16 for this girl Camille earlier in the evening before the Carson family party, so some kids went there first. Jake was tired, so he went home after the Sweet 16, but Sherelle, Emma, and Marybeth just never showed up. According to Kevin, they didn't make it to the Sweet 16 either, and I think he was bothered because he implied that they were out drinking together. At this point, I don't care. I invited them, and if they're not courteous enough to respond or call, then that's their problem.

Teresa

Dec19 (11:15 p.m.)

Dear Diary,

My mom thinks I'm crazy. Like today, I didn't do much. I just sat around my room. She thinks there's something wrong w/me because sometimes when there's nothing to do, like tonight, I sit at home at night on the weekend. She thinks I have some problem or something.

I was talking about this on the phone w/Stephanie and surprisingly (to me) she doesn't do things some nights either. I was surprised because I really thought she was out all the time, but she said sometimes she has nothing to do and that means staying home. Even though she has a boyfriend, sometimes she'll even just stay home to sleep. I can relate to that.

Sometimes I'll call everyone to do something and it

turns out that not one single person is home. Or sometimes I will blow everyone off because I am just so sick of hanging out w/the same people over and over again.

My mom thinks that it's weird for any 16-year-old to be home on a Saturday night. I guess I see where she's coming from, but it's not like my staying home always means I am depressed or anything. Sometimes I'm just not in the mood to be social. I don't think parents understand how busy we are w/school, college stress, grades, SATs, sports, etc. It gets tiring. We need a break sometimes.

marybeth

December 19th

Is it possible to still be wiped out from my basketball game yesterday? By the way—*WE GOT DESTROYED*. At the beginning of the second half we were still in single digits. We were lucky we got as much as we could. My coach only put me in for like 2 min. at the end. I did good even though I was only 0 for 2. Hopefully I will improve on my shooting soon.

All I feel like doing is crashing. And after the game last night I didn't want to go out or go to Camille's Sweet 16 or to Katie's Christmas party or do anything at all. So I watched *Top Gun*. That movie is so awesome. "I feel the need, the need for speed!" Well, not exactly. I think being a pilot must be sooo hard. I am not that smart.

Mom thinks maybe I am still really messed up about the whole fight w/my brother Mitch. Maybe I am. All I know is that I am still not talking to him.

And I'm not talking to Matt either.

Kevin

So this is really messed up, this whole shopping thing. Going to the mall this time of year is like torture I swear. Everyone is pushing and running around at the last minute. It was so awful today. I went w/Adina and even the traffic there and back in my car *SUCKED*. The only thing that's good is that I got everything I needed to get.

Something very strange is the fact that last nite I had to babysit for Zoe, which was like a totally out of the blue request from my mother. I agreed to do it b/c she seemed real stressed and so I just said that sure, I would help. For some reason today I feel like leftovers, kinda chewed up w/out much energy. I always feel that way after babysitting. I dunno how Marybeth and Emma do it all the time for their kid brothers and sisters and cousins. Oh well, I'm tired now so I'm out. Ta ta

Emma

I was exhausted tonight but decided to go online anyway and while I was on, the weirdest thing happened. My old boyfriend Chuck IM'ed me. We were online at the same time. Now this is very bizarre because I haven't even thought about him since the beginning of junior year. I mean, of course I have thought of him, but we just hadn't spoken since I saw him play soccer last fall with that *UGLY GIRL* he was dating.

Anyway, the truth is that we never "officially" broke up, we just sort of drifted apart. And I still wanted to stay friends with him, but he moved to another town. I think maybe Marybeth has talked with him, but not me. I wonder if him talking to me online means we can be friends again. We didn't say much, he just wished me happy holidays and stuff like that. He said he was going skiing with some kids from his school. He did ask if I had a boyfriend, but I played that one down. I didn't want to get into the whole thing with Cliff. And speaking of Cliff, I spent last night with him because he was having a party at his house with soooo many people there. Everyone was drinking beer and even though *I HATE BEER*, I drank some last night. I don't really remember a lot of what went on. We were all so funny and drunk. My cousin picked me up and she took me to the Silverado Diner to get food and mints because my breath still smelled of beer. Thank God she came to get me because I never would have been able to sneak in past my dad. She's cool too. She won't rat me out.

p.s. When we were at the Silverado, we saw Sherelle and Bobby and they were drunk too. Sher could barely walk, she practically tripped over her own feet. She was laughing so hard because I don't think she's ever seen me like that before.

Jake

December 20

Saturday I was supposed to go drinking up the street, but my neighbor went someplace else with the liquor. Oh well, that was that. I went over to Micky Geffen's house and hung out with him and his sister Betsy.

Right now I'm in my bedroom lying next to this stuffed moose that Claudia bought for me. There's a Lauryn Hill song on the radio and it's making me sad. It's "Doo Wop" and she's saying something like, "Guys, you know you better watch out. Some girls, some girls are only about that thing, that thing, that thing." That's for sure—at least in Claudia's case.

It sucks.

Favorite Sounds

<u>Jake:</u>
  <u>Fave sound:</u> Horn honking
  <u>Fave song:</u> Any house music
  <u>Fave lyric:</u> "It's gonna be a party, y'all." —R. Kelly, "Home Alone"

<u>Teresa:</u>
  <u>Fave sound:</u> The pitter-pat of rain and all kinds of music!
  <u>Fave song:</u> Anything from Mariah Carey (she is sooo awesome!)
  <u>Fave lyric:</u> "Though hope is frail, it's hard to kill. Who knows what miracles you can achieve when you believe?" —Mariah & Whitney Houston, from "When You Believe"

<u>Baxter:</u>
  <u>Fave sound:</u> Anything as long as it's not quiet—I hate that
  <u>Fave song:</u> Anything by Britney of course
  <u>Fave lyric:</u> Anything Britney sings of course, and Ace of Base songs

55

Favorite Sounds

Marybeth:

  Fave sound: Good music + the noise babies make

  Fave song: ANYTHING BY DMB (Dave rules!) and Jewel, my idol

  Fave lyric: " I wish you would step back from that ledge my friend. You could cut ties with all the lies. That you've been living in . . ."-Third Eye Blind

Billy:

  Fave sound: Big-time partying!!!

  Fave song: Listen to All-4-One when I do homework

  Fave lyric: "I'd be a fool to surrender when I know I can be a contender."-Coolio

Katie:

  Fave sound: The ocean

  Fave song: "This Is the Moment," from the musical Jekyll and Hyde

  Fave lyric: From Jekyll and Hyde "I won't look down, I must not fall! This is the moment, the sweetest moment of them all"

Favorite Sounds

Kevin:

   Fave sound: FAST CARS And
lAughter

   Fave song: LAtin house music best
of All

   Fave lyric: OKAy, there's like A
million. "The sky is the limit And you
know thAt you keep pressin' on—" from
Notorious B.I.G. AKA FRAncis the
PRAying MAntis, or mAybe even, "I
cAn't get no sleep. . . . InsomniA.
PleAse releAse me." ThAt's by
FAithless on Reverence, or "My love is
All I hAve to give," by the
BAckstreet Boys

Emma:

   Fave sound: The bell at the end of
school

   Fave song: "Have You Ever," by Brandy

   Fave lyric: Anything that can make me
cry

Billy

Now that it's late Dec., I can admit that I'm glad football's over. The season was tough. I mean, there were some good parts, like when we would ride back from games on the bus, especially coming home from a victory. We'd really cut loose. On the way to a game, we would always have to hold everything in and keep it tame but coming back was another story. It's like total chaos—and the coaches allow us free rein on almost everything. After a victory, everyone on the team chants and sings songs and throws each other around on the bus like a bunch of baboons. Me, Deke, Benjamin, and Anthony throw water at and make fun of any kid we think is a nerd or fat. Best of all, we make jokes the whole way. We do chants and the entire bus just bursts into laughter. I can't stop laughing.

But that's all over. Hey, it's not like we had a winning season. A heck of a lot more bus rides were spent angry b/c we fucked up and lost. So it's a mixed memory, let's put it that way. As I've said, I would *much* rather be playing lacrosse. That would be a cool bumper sticker for my car: I'd Rather Be Playing Lacrosse. I have to get one of those.

Gotta get some gifts for people before it's too late but I haven't got any cash. This could be a problem.

Teresa

Dec 20 (9:41 p.m.)

Dear Diary,

Oh well, yet another day where I just stay home and do nothing, just like yesterday. Mom seems less worried about me today. I, on the other hand, am *more* worried. Staying home today was not my free decision. I wanted to go somewhere but didn't have a plan. And of course no one was home when I called. And it was *me* who did all the calling. Why doesn't anyone call me to make a plan? I hate that. Like what is Zach waiting around for? He should call me!!! Do I have a Keep Off sign on my head or what? I mean, I know Leonardo was like a one in a million shot in the dark, but you'd think Zach would at least make a teeny bit of effort. Why do I have such bad guy luck?

Anyway, it's Sunday late and tomorrow's a biggie so I'd better get the homework done. Only 5 more days until Christmas! Ho! Ho! Ho!

Katie

December 20
@ 10:43 P.M.

Here's what I got everyone for Christmas presents:

Mom & Dad: A hand-carved nativity set

Gramps & Grams: A stuffed Santa that plays music, "The First Noel"

Patti: An Abercrombie & Fitch sweater
Paul: 2 CDs and a talking Flick toy from *A Bug's Life*
Sherelle: A Contempo Casuals shirt
Jaclyn: Sterling silver bracelet
Gwen: Estée Lauder makeup kit w/free tote bag
Brad: Electronic compass for his car, a diving watch, and a *new* key to his heart since he lost the first one

I wonder what Brad got for me? He keeps teasing me because he knows I will get excited about whatever it is. Today we spent the afternoon together. I had to write a creative essay for Ms. Gifford's English class. I was working over at his house for a while and his puppy is so cute. He has a basset hound named Trixie. She's all droopy and sad, but it's so cute. And Brad is so gentle with animals—just like he is with me.

When we were together, Brad asked me a question that I've been expecting he would ask for the last three and a half months since we started dating: *Did you ever really love Robert?* He and I have never really talked about our old relationships in a lot of detail. He only knows *some* of the Robert story (not *everything*, not the truth about the hitting part). So he asked and I decided it was best to answer him with complete honesty. I could have told him "no," but that would have been a lie. When I was with Robert, I *thought* I was in love—and obviously I was wrong. Of course love with Brad is a completely different thing. It's just there. I don't even have to think about it that much. Oh, it's late and I'd better get to sleep.

BIG audition tomorrow!

Baxter

December 20

I bought Megan a Christmas present. I got her perfume, CK One. I hope she likes it.

Tonight I beeped her. Of course, she didn't call me back.

Am I ever going to get even 1% of what I want as far as Megan goes? Somehow I doubt it, but I'm not ready to face that yet. So I'll keep beeping.

p.s. Tonite I was talking to Marybeth on the phone and it was sooo funny. Her mom made chocolate chip cookies with M&M's and they came out flat. We were laughing for hours.

marybeth

December 20th

I just got off the phone w/Bax and he was like cracking up at everything I said. What a funny kid. He's always in a good mood. Unlike me these days.

Unbelievable fact #1: Rick Wright called me last night. I was like, "What is going on?" I think b/c it's

61

the holiday season, suddenly everyone has it in 4 U. First Matt, now this.

I could *NOT* believe Wright called me. So I acted all pissy on the phone and he said it was really clear that I did not care what he had to say. I mean, I tried being nice for a while. I did say hello to him in the hall and he was the one who dissed me. And then he said how sorry he was for being mean and I was like . . . too little, too late, buddy.

Unbelievable fact #2: I still am not talking to my brother Mitch. I don't fool around. When I say something I *REALLY* mean it. What a loser.

My mom actually told me she understands me and Mitch. She says that it's okay for me to dish it back to him. She volunteered to talk to him, but I told her not to bother. He won't care. I really wish he would just go away sometimes. Usually when he pulls this stuff w/me I can walk away and blow it off but for some reason this time it's affecting me more. It reminds me of a quote I love:

All my sins . . . I said that I would pay for them if I could come back to you. All my innocence is wasted on the dead and dreaming.—"Angels of the Silences," by Counting Crows

Emma

I had a dream about school last night. Isn't that strange? I'm ready for this week of activities. I'm ready for the break too, actually, but there's a lot to do first. Today I am feeling fine considering how drunk I was on the weekend.

Now this is weird. I got this note from Sherelle today during class that said how psyched she was to see me up at the Silverado over the weekend, and that over vacation she thinks that the two of us should do some drinking and bonding. When she handed me the note in class, I was expecting her usual, "Are you mad at me? If you are . . . why not just tell me?" I mean, usually she writes me notes that are nasty, going off on me before I even have a chance to defend myself, but instead she sends me this one about how much she wants to hang out. What's up with that?

So anyway, I showed the note to Marybeth since we were just talking the other day about Sherelle being different lately and only hanging with Bobby and always changing her mind and making plans without us. And I said, doesn't it seem weird to think that suddenly Sherelle wants to be all buddy-buddy, right? Marybeth agreed and said it must be manipulation somehow. Sher almost NEVER calls Marybeth or me anymore. And it is especially shocking that she asked me to go anywhere with her *alone*. I decided to leave a message on her machine to see if she really wants to hang out or not. After all, she may have already changed her mind. Whatever.

Baxter

December 21
Megan looks so pretty whatever she's wearing, I swear. I saw her this morning and she had on this blue sweater. Why do I like her so much? I really hope she likes the CK One perfume I got her. I think she will. I hope she will. I'm keeping my fingers crossed for Christmas.

Teresa

Dec 22 (7:00 p.m.)
Dear Diary,
The Christmas spirit is really in the air! Here's what's up with my life lately. Things have taken a turn for the *BETTER*!!!

Things with Zach are going great now. ♥ *He finally called.*

I can't stop thinking about winter break—there's so much I wanna do!

64

I've decided that I still have a thing for Kevin (just a little bit but it's there) and am wondering if I should tell him?

There was nothing too special about school announcements or anything this morning. History was boring and I almost fell asleep a couple of times. But English was awesome. *I LOVE MS. GIFFORD!* I know Billy hates this class and he is always bitching about it, but I don't hate it at all. Right now we're reading *A Farewell to Arms,* by Ernest Hemingway, and I participated a lot! Later I had math and physics, which are both harder, but I am happy that I have almost an A average in both so far this year. Oh yeah, and we had SAT review 6th period too. I can't believe that SATs are coming up! When did we get to be this old?! Anyway, that's school. Looking good!

I just woke up from a nap. I crashed when I got home at 3:30. Now it's 6. I guess I'm not getting enough sleep at nite, but who cares. Naps are nice.

p.s. My Spanish teacher says that me and my friend Stephanie are the best in the class! We're getting honors for it!

Jake

December 22

Life still really sux. I received a progress report in the mail from the school and it says that I am doing bad in Spanish class. And that pisses me off a little. It's not that I am doing bad, it's just that I am lazy in Spanish class. Christmas is coming and I still haven't done any shopping. I'm gonna have a lot of trouble since it's only 3 days away. And I have a lot of studying. I wish it were Friday already.

Kevin

12/22

Only Tuesday and all I'm doing is taking freakin tests all week. It's Christmas week—can't they cut us a break? Like I had a chem test this week and I don't know if I did really good or really bad. Right after school today there was a swim meet and we got KILLED. I can't believe how bad we got beat. The coach was pissed b/c our score was only like 34 and the other team's was over 100! So after swimming I went to Vito's for some pizza w/Jake and he was bummin out about shit. Like of course he is. Life is pretty hard for him right now. Ok, I'm out to study. Ta ta

p.s. Oh yeah, almost forgot about life guarding too, which for some reason is *harder* all of a sudden. I mean today Jake told me that we have to learn new stuff before the end of the year. Like I'm really gonna remember all this crap when I dive in the water to save someone.

Marybeth

I don't remember why I like Matt. I really don't. In school today I saw him and he was like telling me how he wasn't mad, which I know is just the biggest LIE. He was supposed to call me and he didn't and I know what's really going on.

The thing is that we were talking on e-mail the other day believe it or not and I told him all the stuff that happened w/my brother Mitch. I expected him to be understanding and take my side but that's not what happened. Okay, what happened next is that Matt started being a real jerk. I mean, I asked him straight out if he was listening to me and all he could do was crack jokes and say mean stuff like getting loud online like when you type in all capital letters. I can't stand that he is ALWAYS jokin' around. He wonders why I always say he is so mean but what am I supposed to say to someone when they're always saying stuff like "Oh, just bite me" to me?

The thing about Matt is that he's always making these sexual jokes to me. Like I was telling him about the fact that I might get a tongue ring (well, I might!)

and all he could say was that it was too bad I had no one to use it on. Like gross—I don't need to hear that from U!! Why do I like him?

The truth is I guess I can't stop talking to him or seeing him b/c he's really the only one I know who's as much of a wiseass to me as I am to him. So I can't let go of the idea of him. So whatever. The end of our e-mail was like *REALLY BAD* because he seemed really mad at me or something. I thought he was the only person I knew who wasn't judging me but maybe he was. I just don't know anything anymore.

To make matters worse all around, I got totally ignored in our 2nd basketball game, which made me so mad. I was the only one on the team who didn't play. I am planning to say something to Coach Vozar tomorrow. He's my math teacher and my basketball coach and now he is my *TOTAL* enemy. I think what he did was really wrong.

2 Bad & I hope *EVERYTHING* gets better fast. . . .

Katie

December 22
@ 10:40 P.M.

I have never acted or sung better in my whole life than I did yesterday. I nailed the audition for *The Boy Friend*! But here's something awful. When I left the audition room to go back to my locker, who was standing in the hallway but *ROBERT*! He looked *disgusting*. And later I found out that the reason he was there was because he coached *Rachel Ross* on her audition! I can't believe that he would prep her to get the lead! I hate the fact that she is still friendly w/him. And what an immature move against me. Oh well, I guess I'll do even better—out of revenge! I am sure Robert was thinking he could make me succumb to nerves by seeing him there—but it *DID NOT WORK*. And there is no way I will speak to Rachel about it. I won't give her the satisfaction!

The only thing is that the drama coach, Remmers, is not posting the parts until lunch tomorrow, when he told us it should have been today. I am so so so nervous. What am I going to do? Good night!

p.s. I almost forgot! I aced my chem test and math test today. Yeah for me! School is going really well—thank goodness.

Teresa

Dec 23 (10:50 p.m.)

Dear Diary,

Since it's the week of Christmas, I have officially decided to blow off all stressful thoughts—especially ones about tests! And especially since I think I may have messed up on a chem test, thanks to Mr. MacTaggart. My horoscope for this week says:

It's the holidays, and you've got people to see, places to go, and things to do—and you

don't want anyone reining you in! Wear red, show off, and get loads of attention! You've got a planetary push coming for the end of the year. Take advantage of it. You are totally in the know—and on the go. Getting along with classmates can boost your GPA.

Yeah, right! I need a good chem grade, not a new friend, to boost *my* GPA!

Every year at this time though my mom takes me & Vincent out to dinner with her and her best friend Maddy and Maddy's daughter Lou (short for Louise). Tonight we went to this really nice restaurant for dinner. Well, as *soon* as we stepped into the doorway of the restaurant, like right away I noticed this *HOT* guy! Oh my God!

I didn't think there would be a chance in a million of us sitting next to him b/c my mom pointed to the other section (on the complete other side of the restaurant) to sit. But thankfully there was no room on the other side so we sat right by the guy! And as the waitress walked past the guy on the way to our table my brother *STOPPED* and said, "Hey, how's it going?" It turns out that he works w/this guy! So Vincent says that the guy's name is Paul Pringle. I thought that was so funny I wanted to laugh right there but then I figured who cares what his name is. Anyway, I am going to remember that name definitely. I can't forget a cute face! Plus I know for a fact that my brother has the list of names and #s of *everyone* he works with! Maddy leaned over to me at one point to say that she thought Paul was looking at our table and I got a little self-conscious eating my spaghetti, like food was all over my face or something, but oh well. Dinner was really yummy as always.

Kevin

12/23

So now it's like Wednesday and it's snowing and today school was funny. Math test 1st period yes it sucked having *ANOTHER* test ok then but the 7th period history test was *EASY*. The funniest part though was these psycho friends of mine. All of us decided at lunch to have a lot of fun since it's the last day before vacation and so we wanted to start this food fight except no one wanted to get dirty. So it wound up only being two kids who did it and they were throwing all this stuff everywhere but then they got into trouble. It was so stupid it was funny. I am so glad today is the last day before vacation—yesssssss!

Baxter

December 23

There was a semi–food fight at lunch although it was pretty immature and the people who started it

71

got suspended. That just seems like a stupid thing to me.

And today I had a lousy physics exam, which stinks. I guessed on so many answers. I didn't know anything. I hope I got more than 15 right, that way I can maybe get some extra credit. After I left class, I met up with friends. Everyone is *so* filled with the holiday spirit.

As far as gifts go, Jessica liked her Beanie Baby (I got her Stretch) and Teresa loved her lollipops. Megan was *BEGGING* for hers (the perfume) but I purposely left it in my locker. The reason I did that was so she wouldn't open it up in front of her friends and in front of me. And as it turns out, she didn't because she was late for her bus so she just ran out of school and said she would open it at home.

I don't even know if she liked it because she hasn't called me. What else is new?

Billy

12-23

I'm not in the mood for Christmas. I don't have gifts and everyone else is swapping stuff at school and I think that's pretty stupid. I saw Bax today and he was giving his gifts to all the girls. What a kiss-up. Talk about technique—ha ha. I don't have to buy girls anything. I considered maybe getting Blair D.

something a *long* time ago but things have definitely changed since then. I think they all look so stupid oohing and aahing about their stupid presents. Especially Bax, who can't get his mind off that one girl Megan Randall. Christmas choir is ok but I really can't get into this Santa shit.

By the way, I think I'm gonna be in the school musical. My name was on the parts list, which was posted this afternoon. It's just chorus but I do get to sing and dress up. I love to sing almost as much as lacrosse. Some other guys from the team made the play too. It should be a blast. The only part of football I was missing was hanging with the team all fall. Now I can see them all winter too. Oh yeah, Katie got one of the leads.

Katie

December 23
@ 6:50 P.M.

I GOT A LEAD IN THE MUSICAL!!! I found out late today. It's actually *not* Polly, the lead I thought I would get, but it's just as good and really the best and most challenging female part in the play in my opinion. I wanted them to cast me against type too because I am so tired of always being the goody two-shoes! At first when I saw the casting list I read the name next to the character *Polly* first and I saw Rachel Ross! I was sooo bummed and figured that I had been put into the chorus. And then I checked the chorus list and saw that they didn't have any second sopranos listed either. Obviously they had just forgotten me!

But then I saw my name next to *Mme. Dubonnet* and I was so psyched! I think it may have fewer lines but it is *SUCH* a better part. She's the headmistress at the boarding school and since it takes place on the French Riviera in the 1920s, I get to put on this thick accent and flirt like crazy with everyone and act all stuffy—it will be so much fun! I am so happy to be cast as something different than me. It is way too easy to just play Polly. I am sooo happy about how things turned out! I knew it would. I have the esteemed privilege of being able to attempt a twist in my own character and people always say the *best* actors are the ones who are cast in the older roles. I'm determined to do well!

Right now it is snowing, which makes today just perfect, and I am so thrilled I don't even know what else to say.

Emma

12/23, 11:35 PM

I feel like it is *really* winter and Christmas because it's snowing tonite. The white looks so beautiful, like it's shining under the moon. Everyone in the house is asleep right now except me. I just got off the phone with Cliff. I ❤ him!

Tonite there was a hockey game and the Bulldogs *WON*! I was so excited. And it was so cool because one of the hockey players' moms got the four managers gifts. I was so shocked. I didn't expect to get anything! She got us each these clear bags w/this strawberry cream and shampoo. And it had some of those beads in it too, like you put in the water when you take a bath. They smell sweet.

This lady is just so nice. Last year she gave me one of those mini–photo albums because she said I did such a good job for her son and the whole team. I never told the other girls about it because I knew they'd feel bad. I mean, I got something and they didn't and I didn't want them to feel left out. Anyway, this lady's son is also really nice and more than that he is so *HOT*! This guy is so hot that we are all like *OBSESSED* with watching him on the ice. Of course he is only a freshman, but we tell him how cute he is *all the time*. He probably hates it but who cares because he is so hot! And anyway, who wouldn't be into the idea of 4 junior girls crushing on you when you're only a freshman! It is just so funny.

Crushes Crushes Crushes

Emma:

I have had crushes on many people but I always keep it to myself just in case that person doesn't like me back. I don't want to get rejected right out in the open where everyone can see. And if a kid likes me and I don't like him, I will say that nicely so he doesn't get embarrassed either. That hurts too much.

Kevin:

Like 4 or 5 times I crushed on different girls but by the time they liked me I liked our friendship better, like (1) Deb, but she wouldn't give me the time of day literally until like this year and now she dates Lazlo so that's iced, and (2) my friend Cristina, who I still crush on a little but I don't really think that she could love me as much as I loved her so it wouldn't have lasted anyway, and (3) Sherelle, who I was crushing on last summer

Crushes Crushes Crushes

even though she BASiCAlly lAughed
it off, And (4) Rosie, who is one of
the other ones I hAve cRied oveR,
like she soRt of bRoke my heARt And
sometimes I still think About her.
And of couRse (5) AdinA, whose
stAtus is wAy up in the AiR Right
now.

Katie:

People have had crushes on me many
times, but the one time that really stands
out for me is when I took this guy to
the semiformal last year. His name is
Patrick Miccelli, a boy I have known
since I was born. I thought I made it
clear that we were going as _friends_ only,
but obviously I didn't make it clear
enough! He kept trying to hook up with
me all night! And the crush continued for
weeks with him calling me and asking me
out. I just could never see him in a
romantic way. I still remember him as the
kid who gave me chicken pox in
kindergarten!

Crushes Crushes Crushes

Baxter:

I'm more of a crusher. Just look at Megan. But I hope that being a crusher doesn't <u>always</u> mean I get crushed. That means my heart would be broken a million times. I don't think I can take that.

Teresa:

I guess I like crushing on cute guys when I see them or meet them like at hockey games or at parties hanging out, but it just seems that the guys I do find don't want me or have girlfriends or whatever. Even when I do hook up it's like only for a short time and that's the extent of it. I probably will never be in love at this rate! Of course, I still think about Kevin sometimes because we just click so much but he is in NO WAY crushing on me so I'd better give up and fast on that one! And of course when I can't find someone in real life to crush on, there's always the movies! How

Crushes Crushes Crushes

can I not have a crush on
Leonardo DiCaprio? He is sooooo
cute.

Billy:

I don't consider looking at a hot girl as
having a crush on her but if I did, I would be
guilty of doing it like every day. I am ALWAYS
checking out hot girls at school and at games. I
can't see the point in getting all emotional and
mushy about it though. In a lot of ways I think
crushes are a big waste of time. Either you like
someone and you tell them or you don't.

Marybeth:

When I have been crushed on, it felt
weird. I felt awkward toward them. Like I
didn't want to be too nice b/c I didn't
want them to get the wrong impression. Or
maybe I am supernice, like the other
extreme. I feel so bad for them b/c I
don't like them. It's hard too when
someone who likes you gets a little

Crushes Crushes Crushes

intense, kind of like what happened w/me &
that kid Rick Wright. As far as having
crushes on other people, I think that
mostly sux. It's okay for a short time,
just as long as you don't get to the point
where you start STALKING the person.

Jake:

Well, I don't really think that many
girls have ever had a crush on me, but
this year Diana Russo did and I hooked
up w/her. But now I feel like I only like
her as a friend. I have had TONS of
crushes where it was the other way
around and the girl only liked _me_ as a
friend. I don't like how that feels. Even
though we used to go out, I still think
about Claudia and so I would say that
right now I have a crush on her. Having
a crush is wanting something you can
never have.

Jake

December 24

Well, it is Christmas Eve and it's hectic. Too much shopping. I just finished my shopping today at the very last minute. I did it! The malls were packed. Of course I was a nut in the mall, making a fool of myself and cracking jokes about everything and everyone I saw there.

Nothing is good in my house right now. My uncle Charlie called and said he wouldn't be coming over on Christmas because of what happened with Frankie, for obvious reasons. My older brother Nate is fighting with Mom and screaming and then my mom gets upset. He is an asshole sometimes about stuff. He would disagree of course. He just thinks I get mad at stupid shit, but he's wrong. I have my reasons.

Like Christmas. I spent like $200 on my family this year. He didn't spend anything.

I hung out w/my dad tonight. He always loved this time of year. We would make snowmen and stuff. This Christmas things are different, that's for sure.

Baxter

December 24

Today was no different than other Christmas Eves have been—lazy, lazy, lazy and *GREAT*. I just sat around, played Nintendo 64, and helped Dad wrap Mom's gifts. Mom made a big dinner too. We had roast beef, mashed potatoes, carrots, gravy, and homemade bread, my mom's special recipe, which is the *BEST*. After dinner I used my new razor to shave and then I went over to Emma's house. Sherelle was actually there with the rest of Emma's family. I was rubbing Sher's feet and everyone made this big deal out of it. Nothing really grosses me out though.

Later we exchanged cards and Emma's was really nice. This is what she wrote. It means a lot.

Baxter,
This card makes me think of something stupid you would say. When I read it I thought of you right away.

Your house smells like something's burning, but it's not.

82

Hun?

Well, where do I start? We have been through so much together and I think you are the only one who knows the most about me. Whenever I am sad or need someone to talk to, you are there for me even if it's just to listen. You have no idea how much that means to me. In fact, I remember the first time we ever talked and all the stuff we went through in middle school. Here we are now, juniors in high school, getting ready for college in a year and you joke about going away to England or something but I swear I won't let you go! I don't know what I would do without you here. You are my BEST friend in the whole world and never forget that. Thanks for always being here for me. Okay, now I am crying so I have to stop writing! I love you! xoxoxoxxo Emma

Katie

I am so in love with Brad and I am *SO* relieved right now. When I finally crawled into bed last nite at 1:30 I was really worried. Brad was supposed to call when he got in at 11:30 but he hadn't and with the snow outside I couldn't help but think the worst. Then at 2 A.M. he called—thank goodness. I was wide awake, almost expecting it. He told me that he had gotten into a car accident, crashed into a fire hydrant after skidding in the snow. He's fine of course but I immediately started crying while he was telling me because I was so relieved. I realized in that moment how much I need him. But of course, I'm not dependent on him.

Today Mom and I are going shopping together for last minute gifts. Tonight we're opening presents together as a family. Last night was for me and Brad. I can't believe I found this guy—I am so lucky. He put so much thought into everything he got for me. They were by far the *MOST THOUGHTFUL* gifts anyone has ever gotten for me. First, he got me a Furby, and then he got this heart-shaped locket and necklace with both of our photos in it. That is so beautiful! He is also going to get us both tickets to go see a play together (he said I can pick the show!) and as if that weren't enough already, he got me a gorgeous ornament with Belle from *Beauty and the Beast* on it. It was pretty cute!

Last year, all Robert got for me was a stupid picture frame. I mean, I liked it but it was just so boring and thoughtless. I think Brad is perfect in every way. Besides, last Christmas Eve, Robert and I got into this *HUGE* fight and he said all these mean and cruel things to me and I was so upset I just crawled into bed and cried. When I look at videos from last year, I see myself looking like a zombie. I really hit an all-time low last December. I will *NEVER* get as low as I was 364 days ago! I will *NEVER* let a boy hurt me that badly again by giving him so much control over what I feel or think. I am my own person now.

10:25 P.M. later on Christmas Eve!!

I am so tired right now! After dinner tonight I went over to Emma's house for a little while. We haven't actually seen each other very much these last few weeks, so it was nice to talk. I have been so busy and distracted lately! So when she called and asked I said of course! Baxter was there too, and Sherelle too. Bax was rubbing her feet—it was disgusting! But we laughed a lot together and played with my new Furby. Merry Christmas Eve!

Kevin

12/24

Okay, so now it is like Christmas Eve for real and I am psyched but I have to say that yesterday really freaked me b/c the shit really hit the fan the exact second I got home from school. Okay, this is it: I go home to take a shower and then my 'rents inform me that my BFF Randi, her gramma died, so I was like "wow" and decided I should go see if I could help her—like go to the wake or something. Even though I *loathe* those things I think it would mean a lot to her and I wanted to help or whatever. So after the wake it's like late & I get home and see that Adina had beeped me like 3 different times. So I called her back obviously but said I couldn't talk b/c I was starving and wanted to eat my dinner. I said I would call her and see her later on that nite. Okay. So then I was surprised b/c my friends showed up. It was Geffen & his sister, Jonny, Jake, and Cristina too. We chatted and decided to watch a movie. By this time it was like 10 already so I called Adina back and said what happened and told her that I probably couldn't come pick her up b/c I thought I would just chill w/my friends. I just didn't feel like going all the way to her house to get her and having to drive all the way back later on. So *THEN* she lays into me like attacking me about how I didn't come by and how I never want to see her now and why did I go to my friend Randi's wake and not go to her uncle's wake. First off, I didn't know her uncle even *DIED* so I dunno where she was going w/that one. I was really livid about her attitude, which made me madder the longer I talked w/her on the phone. So by now my friends are like what is going on and they wanna take off and I'm like no stay please go watch TV or something. Anyway, I am soooo sick of her paranoia about me and what I am doing. It's frustrating having someone be that way w/you. These arguments drive me crazy. So basically I have decided now that Adina and I are like *NOT* working out at all. I think I definitely want to break up w/her but it's like Christmas Eve and I would feel like such a jerk doing it now or tomorrow, even tho she doesn't celebrate Xmas b/c she is Jewish. I don't wanna ruin anything here. So I don't know what to do & I need help. Ta ta for now, K

p.s. the only good thing today = snow

Billy

12-24

Lee is home and we were playing touch football in the snow all morning and that was the best part of the day. He is off somewhere now w/out me. It's Christmas Eve but it's not all that exciting here. Not at all. Maybe I'm just getting a little too old for this kind of thing. Like Baxter always gets so into

Christmas, I don't get why. Well, it's 6:12 P.M. and I have nothing else to do. I have been watching TV like a bum all afternoon but maybe that's not so bad. I mean, sometimes you need that to relax you.

Actually, I know I am supposed to be in the giving mood, but really I am pissed today in some ways. My dad took away my driving privileges. Because of that ticket I got, the car insurance went up $100 every 6 mos. So right now Dad is calling me a probationary driver. If I get one more offense I have to go to driver's school, so Dad thinks I should stay in and not drive at night *especially* if the weather is bad because it will lessen the chances of my getting into any kind of accident or getting another ticket. And there are a lot of extra police out at night too. All I know is that it sux.

This whole holiday is kind of bad for me. I mean, I know it is important religiously and all that, but I don't see the big deal. I didn't get that much anyway from my parents. I feel like I'm missing out in a way. Okay, then, a few more hours of doing nothing left to go. Maybe Lee will come home soon. I wonder if anyone else ever got this bored on Christmas Eve.

Marybeth

It's 7:32 A.M. and I am wide awake and this sux! Anyway, yesterday I gave my BB coach, Mr. Vozar, a big FU. Merry Christmas, Coach.

Here's the story: For all of practice I didn't talk and now I have a black eye because someone's elbow hit me on a rebound. So n e way, at the end of practice when everyone was shooting foul shots I talked 2 Vozar. I was like can I talk 2 U for a minute and he said ok and that's when I tried to be nice and ask him what I was doing wrong. I asked him why I was the only one who didn't play the other day.

So that's when he said to me that he just didn't see an opportunity to let me into the game b/c it was just 2 close. And then I could feel my face start to get hot and upset but I just shook my head. He was like looking right at me and told me not to get my feathers all ruffled b/c I have plenty more chances to play during the season. I have plenty more games to "prove myself." What a bunch of *LIES*! Now I really felt like giving Vozar a big, giant FU. Instead, I was like, you know what Coach Vozar, don't you think there was n e thing that could have been done, especially after our starters threw a 13 point lead? He just shook HIS head and said, "No, Miss Miller, I do not." Just like that, slowly and deliberately, and then he walked away. I was so pissed! I threw my basketball at the bleachers in the gym and went into the locker room. Everyone was like dodging out of my way *REAL FAST*.

So that's a nice way to start Christmas, right? I guess though that things got a little bit better at nite b/c I went to Matt's hockey game and at like halftime or whatever, I saw his mom sitting way over on the other side of our section over near Emma and the other hockey managers. I tried not to look her way, but all of a sudden I hear someone yell my name and when I turn it's her and she's waving at me, like flapping her arms to come over.

When I walked over, she gave me this big hug and asked me if I was having fun and all that and I said of course I was having fun watching her son! Of course that must have been the correct thing to say b/c then she laughed w/me. I also made her laugh when I said that I was absolutely freezing and had to keep ducking out to go to the bathroom. She liked that one!

Apparently, as soon as I walked away, Emma claims that she heard Matt's mom turn to her husband and say something about my pretty hair and how I was the "one" and wasn't I so cute for Matt? I can't believe that she said that! That's good 4 me. It's about time.

Emma

So I have been thinking whether or not it is a good thing, the whole thing w/Sherelle. I think maybe it's time that I dealt with the reality of the situation. I mean, the reality is that Sher doesn't really call me or Marybeth anymore and spends all her time with Bobby. I really *DO* want to hang out, but I hope it's without him. I'm sure it won't be, but I can hope, can't I? Sher is coming over later. I'm having some friends for Christmas Eve and she said she'd come.

I am so glad that Christmas is finally here. I was so excited this morning to be out of school and I can't wait to see what Cliff got for me! I really hope he likes what I got him. I got him cologne like this aftershave stuff that he wears and 2 T-shirts because he said he needed more to sleep in. What he really said was that he would like whatever I got for him, no matter what it was. He is so good like that. And it is *SUCH* a good thing that he came over that other time to meet my family because I would not want him to be uncomfortable. My mom likes him so much, which makes everything a lot better.

There is still snow outside so I guess it really is a white Christmas. And my brother Ronnie is being cute for once—as opposed to how he can be when I'm babysitting, which is like a little troublemaker. Tonight Ronnie wants to wait up and see Santa. He is so excited about him coming to visit. We have this whole routine that we do every year.

1. Leave a key outside because we don't have a chimney

2. Leave out cookies and cocoa (and he asked if Santa reheats the cold cocoa in our microwave, which was hard not to laugh at)

3. Leave carrots for the reindeer. Now I have to still believe in Santa for him. We're all happier. I love looking at Ronnie's face on Christmas when he opens all his gifts. Oh yeah—I almost forgot I got the cutest card in the whole world from Baxter tonite. Here it is.

Hope you get everything you wish for . . .
Before you've even wished it!

Emma,

What's up? I know you know that you are a great friend. You are always there for me, and you know that I will always listen to your problems and try to give good advice. That's enough of the mushy stuff. You probably wrote more on your card to me but that's only because

you write like this!

(just kidding)

Love ya and Merry Christmas,

Baxter

Teresa

Dec 24 (3:00 a.m.)

Dear Diary,

It's Xmas Eve! Well, really it's Christmas already since it's 3 in the morning. I just cannot sleep. I just *CAN'T BELIEVE* that it's Christmas already. I don't know what to do with myself . . . wait for Santa?

I am really looking forward to Mom's Xmas dinner tomorrow with her standard Italian food (like macaroni and lasagna instead of turkey and stuffing). It is sooooo yummy! I used to be really into material things for Xmas but now it's more of a holiday for family and love now or at least that's what I really really want it to be. Love!!!

p.s. But I *am* still curious about what presents I'm gonna get—esp. from Zach. I can't help myself!

Jake

December 25

Christmas is ok. I just opened my gifts though and I didn't get anything I really wanted and really I barely got any presents because of the situation at home with my family. My dad of course can't go out and shop and my mom just doesn't have the time or the money. She had to stay home and take care of my dad. The only good thing about Xmas this year is that at least we were all together.

Katie

So far Christmas Day has been *awesome*! My family is wonderful and we had a great morning. After everything that happened late last night with Brad, I wanted to sleep in as much as possible, but I was awoken by Christmas chamber music blasting through the house. We all opened presents together—and Santa *loves* me! The Carson house on Christmas morning is like no other place in the whole wide world! We have a couple of family traditions that Mom keeps. For one thing, you always wake up with a sticky face (it's where Rudolph gives you a chocolate kiss when he comes into your room in the middle of the night). And of course there's also Mom's recipe for homemade Christmas waffles that always look better than they taste, although I don't think we'll tell her that! She slaves over them dutifully every December 25! My parents really believe in making holidays a big, big deal to the point where you can barely walk across the room, there are sooo many presents in there. I am so thankful for that. I think it brings us together. I must have 30 presents in front of me right now while I am writing this. Here are the top few:

1 Ring with gold flowers and diamonds in the band

2 China doll (my aunt is a big collector, so she

gives me one every year as a keepsake so I'll be a collector too!)

3 Terry-cloth bathrobe and rosewater lotion (my favorite!)

4 A *new journal* that's leather bound—and this cool silver pen

Of course there's other, smaller stuff (the 30 presents include stuff from my brother & sister too).

The funniest Xmas moment all day so far was when my dad and my uncle came in the house with this new puppy! Apparently my uncle is just dog sitting for the neighbors, but for a minute me and Paul and Patti thought we were also getting a doggy for Christmas. I was jumping up and down—but unfortunately the pup is just a visitor.

We all had a blast! My family is better than anyone's, I swear. I am soooo lucky to have them. There are like 20 relatives here, including the doggy!

9:43 P.M.

Okay, it's later. After my family left I got a little bored so I invited over Emma, Marybeth, Sherelle, Baxter, Brad, and Brad's buddy Tim. We just hung out and talked. It's so good to know that no matter what else can happen we can still be as close as we used to be. Anyway, I am exhausted. Merry Christmas! Two more days and we're off to Gramps and Gram's house in Florida. Yeah! It's not the grandpa we have Thanksgiving with, it's my dad's pop, so I haven't seen him and my grandmother in almost a whole year! I am very excited about it. We'll be staying at this really nice hotel resort.

Billy

12-26

Some Christmas. I can't drive for a week now just because I was a half hour late coming home the other night? So I can't *DRIVE* at *all* now?!!

I can't talk about it. I'll flip.

Emma

12/26, 10:55 PM

Wow. The day after Christmas and it went *REALLY* well, if I do say so myself. It started out a little weird because my brother woke me up jumping on me and jumping on the bed and I had a really bad stomachache. But after that went away, I went to open my presents. Santa brought me a new jacket and makeup bag, nail kit, and mo' money!! And then my dad took me today to get a beeper, which was so cool. They remembered! That was *DEFINITELY* my best gift.

We really didn't do anything major during the day except watch TV and stuff. After dinner and all that, I went over to Katie's house with Baxter, Marybeth and

Sherelle, and Katie's boyfriend. Even though her whole family was there, I didn't feel so bad. I've met some of them before. We were talking a lot about memories and stuff. So Christmas turned out ok.

Right now I am sitting here waiting for Cliff to call me. He said he would call me when he got home and that should have been a while ago. We were supposed to hang out. I also called Marybeth and Sherelle and tried to get them. Where are they? I dunno. I remember now that Marybeth has to babysit and I think Sher said she was going to be w/Bobby. Okay. I beeped her—on MY beeper! We'll see if she calls me. I don't really care. Her loss. I'm too tired to hang out anyway.

p.s. In just three days it's me & Cliff's anniversary! I can't believe a whole month has passed!

Kevin

12/26

WELL EVERYONE I KNOW HAS GOT A
REASON TO SAY PUT THE PAST AWAY
—*Third Eye Blind*

Like that doesn't describe my life right now oh man it sure does I am so freakin tired of things staying the way they are so a *LOT* is happening. Ok, here let's start w/Christmas day yesterday since I haven't written about this. Ok. I didn't really get all that I wanted but

I made out good so who am I to complain. I have had a lot going on w/swim team and lifeguarding and school so I didn't pick out stuff so Mom just got me gift certificates to Musicland and shit. I am psyched to get some more CDs for my car. Ok. During the day on Christmas yesterday my family got together and was actually decent. Everyone is pretty much the same as I remember them being last year. And on Christmas Day for a little while things even got better again w/me & Adina b/c she came over to give me my gifts. She gave me a razor and my fave thing peanut M&M's, one of those cartons of them from Price Club—and I gave her the ring and locket I got for her a while ago. For whatever reason when I saw her everything seemed just fine and we were both happy and all and it was cool. Of course, that was like not supposed to stay that way obviously since today everything changed back to the way it was the other day when I was saying how I didn't like her anymore.

Ok, this is what happened. This morning me, Jake, Lazlo, Micky Geffen, and some other guys from the neighborhood went to this cool place in the middle of the woods, this place where we all used to go when we were like 5 years old. It's this clearing where there's a stream and a waterfall and it freezes over so you can skate—it is so cool. Ok. So after that it was late by the time I got back home, like it was already 5 o'clock. And that's when Adina called. She was pissed that I didn't tell her where I was and I said like a million times that I was sorry but she didn't care. And then we hung up and then 10 minutes later she called back again and started asking me what was going on. So I told her about everything. I said we were too different and that I wasn't happy *AT ALL* b/c I was sooo sick of fighting w/her. I said we should be friends. She was upset and kept saying, "So what are you saying?" like she didn't believe this could be happening. I couldn't believe it, actually. So it's officially over now and even though that is horrible, I feel all right b/c better to do it now than later. It's so late now so bye. Ta ta

Marybeth

December 26th

My Christmas could *NOT* have been better. I got a bunch o' stuff including a shirt from Abercrombie & Fitch *AND* a CD player for my car (woo woo woo), money, and other stuff. Christmas night I was a little bored/tired of the whole family scene so I went over to Katie's for a little bit. And that was a surprise! And then today I got an even bigger surprise when Sherelle called me to go to the mall. *THAT* was a shocker! She & I have not really been hanging out that much, so . . .

I've been kinda bummed out about the whole Matt situation. On the 24th I know for a fact he was on the computer and when I IM'ed him, he ignored me. So then I wrote this letter to him just saying hi. I *STILL* have not gotten any response from him. But I guess maybe it's all my fault. To let myself start to like someone like him when I knew going into the whole thing that he already had sorta mixed feelings. Oh well. It sux but I'll live. Although I hate it when my friends all have boyfriends and I have shit. Maybe Matt & I will become just really good friends or something.

p.s. I have not dealt w/the whole Coach Vozar/basketball thing. I don't know if I am going back to practice on Monday.

Baxter

December 26

This morning I heard that Kevin and his gf broke up *on the day after Christmas*! I can't imagine doing that with someone. What's going on around here? I think breakups are truly an awful thing, but I can't say it's a surprise. I have noticed that the two of them lately are very cold. Well, Kevin doesn't seem to be with Adina all the time. He even called me yesterday to see where I'd be this weekend. BIG surprise since no one usually calls. Anyway, she's history.

I was happy because Billy came over today and we played Nintendo 64. I got this cool *South Park* game yesterday, which is addictive. Billy loves it. Then we also watched *Santa Claus: the Movie,* which was pretty stupid. I only really watched the first half hour. I was dozing off. That's probably because I woke up so early yesterday for Christmas. Like a five-year-old I woke up at 6:30 and then rolled over and tried to sleep until 7:50. After 8 I woke up my brother Jerry and we opened up stuff. I watched a parade on TV and ate a lot. It was soooooo much fun and my family was so funny.

Teresa

Dec 26 (12:40 p.m.)

Dear Diary,

I cannot believe what happened to me on Christmas Day! Well, I opened my presents and got TONS of great music including Goo Goo Dolls, Jewel, Jay-T, etc., this awesome new hair dryer (I just burned out my other one!), free *TANNING* (yes!), and a new 10-CD-changer CD player. I was so happy. Who wouldn't be?

Then later on that nite, Vincent had some friends over and most of them are over 20 but there I was talking to them all! And this was the 1st time my brother didn't yell at me to get out or to leave him alone. He just let me hang out with all of them. They are really cool and we enjoy each other's company. *I CANNOT BELIEVE VINCENT COULD BE SOOOO MATURE!!* The funny part was that my mom's friends came over too and so the house was loud, loud, loud! I guess it's ok that I didn't go to Virginia. I had enough fun here.

The only teeny-weeny part that was no fun was that I could've had people over too, but *NO ONE WAS AROUND*. Where did everyone go? I called everyone I could think of but noone answered. Even Zach had other plans, which I expected. He said he'd call tonite or Sunday or something.

All in all it was a fine Xmas. Yeah!

Billy

12-27

I am so psyched to be spending a lot of time together w/my brother Lee. I wish he would be here more than just holidays. I look up to him so much b/c he is the one thing that I am not, which is *NICE*. Nice in all means that he is 20x nicer than I. Of course I am a little nice but he is such a saint that I feel mean when he's around. It's not a bad thing though, I don't think it's bad. I mean I'm not supposed to feel bad, I just happen to notice that I do. Like with the family car. He said I could keep it and have it even though he's the one who's at U Michigan and needs a car. It's like he is totally selfless. I could never be that way. He just does everything for me whenever I need help. No questions asked either.

Like this week he didn't get all over me about the driving thing. He just let it go. I wish I could let go of things instead of dwelling on problems all the time and worrying about whether or not I'm gonna fail out of school or not. I feel like a failure next to Lee, I guess. I wanna be more like him all the time. I wanna know how.

When I Feel Like A Failure

Emma:

This is a big one for me. When I found out that I didn't pass this one English test I felt like the biggest failure alive and I couldn't figure out why it was that I didn't pass and I felt soo dumb. I cried and cried and people kept telling me I wasn't dumb, but they had all passed it so what did they know anyway?

Baxter:

This year I have learned to accept failure. It is really not as bad as I thought it was. It just makes success soooooooooooooooooooooooo much better.

Kevin:

I do fail at some to a lot of things that I try to do but I don't let that get me down I look to the things that I excel in. Usually I look toward having fun more than whether I win or

When I Feel Like A Failure

lose. I set my own goals and am satisfied with what I can do not what other people want me to do.

Teresa:

Failure sucks! Seriously, I feel so let down if I do poorly, like when you try soo hard on something and u end up failing. I'm also afraid of being a failure to a boyfriend or friends in some way. What if I do something wrong? What if I screw up? And what about college? What if I get rejected from my number-one school? Then I would HAVE to settle for second best. Let's hope that doesn't happen!

Billy:

Failure is grades that suck and not having driving privileges—even if I passed my road test w/o mistakes.

When I Feel Like A Failure

Jake:

Failure is hard to deal with when it seems like everything goes wrong no matter how hard you try. Sometimes I feel like a failure when I can't get all my work done in time to see more of my dad.

Katie:

I look at failure in an optimistic way, as something to learn from. Why stress over the negative when you can see the positive?

Marybeth:

U r a failure if u don't believe in urself B4 it's 2 late.

Kevin

So it's Sunday now and a day since the breakup and nothing feels different go figure. I spent most of the day w/my dad. He's got some business trip coming up and he wanted to spend some time together. It was kinda stupid tho b/c we ended up going to this family party (his side) and I am not into that *AT ALL*, I hate it sooo much I just barely know the names of my aunts and uncles and cousins and I am not into hanging out w/them. I mean some of them are cool yes they are but it's mostly just a lot of small talk. I dislike that strongly and I hate how the favorite question is always about school. School sucks, ok? It's like I wanna put a sign on my head that says, "If you're gonna ask me about school *DON'T* cause it sucks and I am not in the mood for meaningless babble w/you ok? So after we got home at like 7 or so I met up w/Jake and went skating (sort of). Zach fell in the pond, which really kicked ass he looked so funny all wet and freezing ha ha! Then until late Jake & I rocked Nintendo 64 playing 007.

Jake

Today I went to this pond near my house. I went w/my friends from the neighborhood like Kevin, my brother Nate, Micky Lazlo, and my pal Zach. Right now Zach is sort of seeing Teresa but she couldn't go w/us—today was just for us *GUYS*.

Okay, so I couldn't ice-skate because my skates don't fit me anymore, but some of the other crew were skating. The pond wasn't totally frozen but good enough in some parts. The wetter parts we called jelly because they would create a wave and swoosh back and forth if you set foot near them. But even though it was maybe a little dangerous, Zach and Nate kept skating over that one part and eventually Zach fell in. The water is only 2 feet deep so he was ok but we were all laughing hysterically. He had to crawl out and he was sopping wet and freezing cold and it was pretty funny. I wish I had my camera so I could take his picture. I did snap a shot of Nate though, who tried to go back to the hole where Zach fell in. Of course, Nate took a dunk too. I got pictures of *that* whole scene. Dad thought the story was funny when me and Nate told him about it at dinner.

Tonite I went over to Kevin's for a game of 007 on Nintendo 64. I think we need to find a new video game though, cause this one is getting old.

Katie

December 27
@ 3:30 P.M.

I feel like an old lady taking naps and sleeping late like this! I slept until 12 today and I am still tired! Brad says it's because I get no sleep at night. Maybe he's right. But I still feel old! Plus I am so behind in everything I need to do. I started packing for Florida yesterday afternoon at 2 or so, and I still hadn't finished by 2 A.M.

Last night Brad and I had a very unusual adventure in the city. First of all, we missed our train and ended up waiting an hour for the next one to come. And then we were supposed to meet up with Brad's mom and dad for dinner and a play, but he forgot his cell phone and so we never found each other! Brad was so embarrassed about messing up that part of the plans. So we ate alone! But everything turned out okay because we found this cool buffet dinner and ate so much food I was stuffed! Brad said his parents would be okay with everything and when we finally did find them (at the theater) they were very understanding. We saw a production of *Les Misérables*. I've seen that play twice live and once on the PBS special and I know every single lyric by heart. I love it so much! What a wonderful treat from Brad!

Even though I will miss Brad so much, I am so grateful to be going away on a minivacation to the Sunshine State! Visiting Gramps and Gram in Florida is usually a lot of fun because we do so much when we're together. He loves spoiling us—and this year, we decided to take a whole week vacation and my pal Gwen and her family are coming with us. Well, I'd better get ready to go to the airport. Our plane leaves a little bit after 6 o'clock. More later.

11:49 P.M.

Here we are at Gramps and Gram's. Actually, we're staying in this really nice hotel in his town of Vero Beach, Florida. It's called the Driftwood Inn and it is right on the ocean. My grandparents have a condo at this development not far from here at a place called the Moorings. It's nice and it's right on the golf course, but there isn't enough room for the five of us. Plus we want to hang out more with Gwen's family. Dad decided to book us at the Driftwood because it has a cool pool and the rooms are right on the water and everything! Actually I feel bad for Gwen because she has a view of the garbage disposal! Oh well. It's also in the middle of the beach town so we can walk everywhere on our own.

It seems so funny (it always does) to see all the Christmas decorations up around here though, especially when it's 70 degrees outside! Christmas lights are on all the palm trees. I can't wait to hang out on the beach with Gwen tomorrow. I think we're going to try scuba this trip. Mom is happy to have Mrs. Hirsh here too. They'll be hitting the outlet malls and going off to Palm Beach, I'm sure.

The only bad thing about the trip is how much I miss Brad. And it hasn't even been 24 hours! I don't know how I am ever going to survive 7 DAYS without him. I can't get over how attached to him I have become. I've never felt this way about anyone before. I think I might call him right now.

Marybeth

December 28th

Earlier today I built up my courage to call Matt even though I said I wasn't going to do that. He was like annoyed at me though b/c I guess he was playing PlayStation and I called at the wrong moment. I was like do u wanna do something later? He was like well I can't really b/c I'm doing something w/my dad. I was like *OH* well, so do u wanna do something tonite? He was like we'll see I dunno. Then we got off. He hasn't called yet but I hope he calls. He still hasn't sent me an e-mail either.

Oh well. Better catch some ZzZzZzs. Vacation is going kinda slow so far. I have to babysit and that's it pretty much. The only big thing that's happening is that Kevin broke up w/Adina. Big news but I don't think it's a bad thing. Bye!

Kevin

Today so far started out bad w/swim practice at like 9 a.m. and I think maybe the coach was pissed b/c NO ONE was into waking up that early on vacation. That's the burden of being in sports though ha ha J/K. I had to do some stuff around the house again today but then a group of us hung out late, which was cool. Anyway, I was kinda pissed off b/c the whole nite Geffen was taking shit from Jonny and it was kinda ugly like no one was in a good mood AT ALL. So I was like what the fuck is your problem Jonny and I went home.

Emma

12/28; 3:13 PM

What is everyone's problem? What, we're out of school for like a couple of days and suddenly no one has any time to do *anything*. Right now I am sitting here at home wearing these cool Tommy Hilfiger pants that Cliff got me for Xmas. I am so bored! I am also watching my soap opera and freezing since I guess these pants aren't too warm. For the past 2 nights I have done NOTHING.

Cliff never called this weekend, like I said. I guess

112

he went out with his friends or whatever. I wouldn't care if that's what he wanted to do but the least he could have done was to call and tell me that. Marybeth was babysitting so she wasn't around. Sherelle claims she never got my beeps all weekend. Whatever. Yesterday she did try to make up for it by calling and saying hi but I was on the computer and wasn't really paying attention to her. I told her I beeped her with 911 but she said, "Really, I never got it." She had some big song and dance about something but I was not in the mood. I knew the whole thing she was saying was a lie. Then we started talking about when we would exchange gifts and we decided it would be today. But Sherelle had a problem with that plan too. I don't understand her *AT ALL*. I finally told her that she could come over now or never basically, since me and Marybeth wanted to get started. She said she couldn't. Oh well, her bad. If she wants her stupid gift she can just come and get it herself. Later. xoxoxxoxoxo

Marybeth stayed for dinner and then Cliff came over later with his friend Josh, who I always talk to online. We played Monopoly but those guys always cheat so me and Marybeth stopped. It was really funny though because Marybeth hates Monopoly so much and she was like complaining the whole time! I could tell Josh was annoyed but I was laughing so hard inside. Cliff looked so cute! At like 11 or so I drove him and his friend back to Cliff's house and then I drove Marybeth home too. Right now I am actually on the phone with Cliff and he is being VERY stupid. He is playing a video game while talking to me and he's so into wanting to beat the dumb game that he is paying no attention to me. I really hope he figures out how to beat the game! Oh well, I'm going to go take a shower. My dad is yelling for me to get off the phone.

Billy

12-28

Thankfully Dad gave me back my driving privileges. He is the best! I know I was begging him to do it and I think he felt bad b/c all my friends were going out on the town and partying for the different holidays and being on vacation. Like I went to a party tonight w/my old football friends. It was great with beer, girls, partying, and everything else great. I had some drinks but I was trying to be careful. I can't afford to get a ticket or get into trouble right now and there's snow on the ground too. Even though it's vacation I feel a little stressed out for no reason. I think maybe it's b/c Lee is home or something. Maybe. I always feel this pressure to do good when he's here. I wonder if he knows how much I want to be like him.

Anyway, tonight was a great release. Being around

my crazy friends it's like this drug that I have to release stress from my life. Who needs real drugs when
you have these guys is what I say. I'm glad to be
hanging out w/them now that we're out of school for
a week.

Teresa

Dec 28 (5:07 p.m.)

Dear Diary,

One week off from classes and that is sooooo
great! The bad thing is that I have homework! *YUCK!*
Right now it is 5:07 p.m. and I am not sure what I am
doing tonite yet. Last nite my friend Gina came over
and we bonded. But what's weird is that *I STILL* have
not heard from Zach. I called him last nite but there
was no answer and I didn't feel like leaving a message.

Yesterday I went to this indoor hockey league that
I go to on weekends. I walked into the place though
and *I SWEAR PEOPLE WERE GIVING ME DIRTY
LOOKS!* It makes me so crazy because I feel that way
all the time. What are they looking at?

Earlier today I went into my brother Vincent's
room and found that list of phone numbers from his
work. I found that kid Paul Pringle's phone # so eas-
ily! Not like I'd actually call him, but it's cool just to
have his #!

Actually, the reason my brother isn't here right

now is because he's over visiting w/a friend of his, this girl Lauren. It was like a year ago when her sister got really really sick and died from this tumor in her head. It was so sad even though I didn't know her very well. I met them a couple of times. Anyway, Vincent was really upset earlier today. I feel bad. Death is such a scary thing. I think about it all the time and how it could affect any of us at any time. Maybe that's why I have a problem with anxiety!! Speaking of which, I wrote this poem in honor of all my weird, insecure feelings that seem to be everywhere overwhelming me these days.

TOO MUCH

Too much time to waste
Too much done in too much haste
Too much locked inside of me
Too much insecurity
I have too much to think about
I have too much pain and too much doubt
I only want to be touched
But maybe I want too much
I want all bad things to go away
I want too much right now today

Katie

It is awesome here in Florida—stress-free and no worries! There are a bunch of people here since it's my family and Gwen's family together. She has 3 older brothers and an older sister Cassie (all are at least 21). Drinking seems to be this big deal but I'm holding up! Tonite when we were having dinner at the club, everyone just assumed we were 21, I guess, and so Gwen was having beer and drinks w/her siblings. Her mother says that's okay. My mom also said I could have a drink or two, but I have no desire to do that. Why do it just because it's there?

Today during the day was really great though. The sunrise over the ocean this morning was awesome. Mom woke me up to see it, even though I crawled back into bed to sleep some more afterward. The sky is so blue. Later on, Gramps and Gram came over for breakfast at the Driftwood and we all decided to spend the afternoon at this Marine Center and then to take this boat ride to this secluded island where they show you alligators. It was in the middle of nowhere and on the way back to the ocean we stopped and saw manatees too. They were migrating! Then on the way home, Gramps gave us a very big surprise—he had arranged for Gwen and myself to spend the late afternoon going parasailing. I have always wanted to do that but I wasn't sure. Of course my brother teased

117

me about the 300-foot drop and then Gwen started talking about shark-infested waters, and I didn't know what to think! When they hoisted us into the air and I was perilously perched on this platform up in the sky waiting for the official "launch," all I could think about was how much I wished I could be sharing this with Brad. I wanted him there so badly at that moment.

Today is my parents' anniversary and I had to remind them—they both forgot. I couldn't believe that!! We left them to have a romantic dinner and had our own dinner with Gramps, Gram, and "the kids." Patti and Paul are the center of attention, of course, since everyone else is so much older. We ate in Gram's favorite restaurant, this really fancy place right on the Indian River (even though I didn't think the food was that good). After dinner I went for a long walk with Gwen and we just talked and talked, which was so nice. We haven't really bonded in a while.

I wasn't sure if I would call Brad tonight, but I did. It was nice to hear his voice. I think he was happy to hear from me too, but I couldn't tell. I'm sure he's enjoying his freedom—I think it's unhealthy to spend every minute together. I feel like we've mastered the balance in our relationship. I think so, but sometimes I get paranoid. Balance is so important in high school relationships—and it is so confusing! I know I shouldn't worry about it but I do—constantly, and it IS important. Once again I realize how I must let my heart step before my brain. I just hope my heart knows where it's supposed to go!

Jake

December 28

I didn't feel like going to work today so I didn't go. It doesn't really matter anyway because there isn't much work on Mondays. So then I woke up at 11:30 and stayed in my bedclothes almost the whole day. I was just lying down and playing Title Soccer on Nintendo 64 because that's what my sister and I like to do together when we're bored over vacations.

Then Kevin called me around 4:00 to see if I could come over so I did. They were doing some work inside the house like painting and asked if I could help and of course I said yes. I would do anything for the Moran family because they do everything for me. That ended at like 7:30 and then me and Kevin called up Mick Lazlo and we went out to Burger King for dinner. BK is such good food.

After dinner, the three of us crashed Jonny's house to play some cards and we watched *Armageddon* together. Now we have seen that movie like 4 different times. At some point we were kind of bored after watching the movie so we started drinking. We all had a tequila mix and found The Playboy Channel since Jonny has cable.

Kevin and Lazlo left at 10:30 because they had a swimming practice in the morning but I didn't leave until 11:30. My mom was real mad at me because she didn't expect to have to pick me up and she was already in bed when I called her.

Baxter

December 29

Right now I am in bed getting over being sick. I was so so so so so so so sick last night! I mean *REALLY* sick. I threw up count it *ELEVEN* times. Yes, 11 times! Ten of which were in a 5-hour range. It was just this bug I must have caught. I could not keep anything down. *IT WAS AWFUL.* Even when there was nothing left in me I threw up the water I was drinking to keep from getting dehydrated and to get the awful taste out of my mouth. After so many trips from bed to the bathroom, I gave up and just stayed on the couch for a while. I am really sore and tired. Getting sick like this takes a lot out of you. Even my eyes hurt along with my chest. I think I will be fine though.

Marybeth

December 29th

I am really tired. I just got in and it's 1:54 A.M.—almost 2 o'clock! Tonight I hung out with Kevin, Jake, Zach, May, and my friend Chris Smith who's back from college for the holidays even though he says he doesn't believe in celebrating them. Oh well! We were all over at Kevin's house and had a blast together. We watched *Lethal Weapon 4* and had a load of fun.

Tonight when I was w/those other guys I realized something very important. Matt is not the right guy 4 me. Not right now at least. All I wanted was a friendship w/him and he has to be such an ass about it all. He like ignores me on AOL and never calls me back when I leave him messages. Who needs a friend like that??! Tonight I had so much more fun w/these friends who are *REAL* friends and who really care about me. Hanging out w/Kevin and Jake is great b/c they make me happy to be me. They make me laugh like nonstop.

Kevin

12/29

So tonite me and Jake and Lazlo and the rest of us were here at my place and even Chris Smith and his cousin Meg dropped by and she is pretty much of a hottie if you ask me. Marybeth came by too b/c she's close buds w/Chris. I didn't realize how much I really miss seeing her! She & I always connect and I can really use a few laughs these days. I don't think she's at a loss or anything about the whole situation w/Adina—she told me that. She said I was fine w/out a chick for now. I don't know about *that* one but we'll have to see what happens. Jake told me the same thing. Anyway we were just all screwing around together a lot watching the movie *Lethal Weapon 4*—it was good quality fun 4 all ha ha. That's basically it though. Ta ta

p.s. I'm getting over Adina quicker than I even thought. It's like it was so intense and now it's more like later for you. It's so weird how shit changes just like *THAT*.

Jake

December 29

Tonite I wanted to go to this local Club Clove because there was this good singer there but I had no ride. So then I thought maybe a group of us could play Nintendo again but no one else wanted to go. So then I went over to Kevin's and played 007 anyway. Then all these other people came over and we all watched *Lethal Weapon 4*. It was ok I guess.

Today seemed like a long day. I had work earlier so I just went. I had 3 leads and then I came home and ate some Wendy's. Not much else. The usual at home w/Mom and Dad and Nate and everyone else.

Katie

December 29
@ 11:00 P.M.

It was a fairly typical day at the beach today . . . if you count typical as sunny and *gorgeous*! I went down earlier than Gwen this morning and got some reading done. I have assignments to read over the break, *Huckleberry Finn* and some other books. The beach is fine in the morning when it's cooler out but later in the afternoon I have to watch out and sit with a hooded jacket and towels over my head & legs. I'm in a lot of pain. For some reason I got a *really bad* sunburn yesterday and I am paying for it today. I can't afford to get any more burnt. Plus I am freezing cold now because I have the sunburn chills! I can't win.

We went shopping later on with the "girls," which means me, Gwen, my mom, and Gwen's mom, Mrs. Hirsh. I wanted to buy so many things! We were at the outlet malls in Palm Beach and Mom insisted I get something special to remember the trip by. I bought a purse and matching key chain (for my new car when

I get my license—I hope so!). I called Brad before dinner tonight to tell him all about our adventures. He thought it sounded sweet.

Tonight was the funniest part of the trip so far. What a story! I was in my hotel room washing up after the long day, and I went to the bathroom. But something broke inside the toilet and the water started rising up. It was so awful because as luck would have it—I have my period. There was nothing I could do to stop the water except put towels on the floor and then I knocked on the connector door in my room because next door is my mom and dad. Dad came in to help but I was even embarrassed to let him in so then he went down to the lobby to get a plunger. Since he must have appeared incapable of completing such a task, he came back a half hour later with a plumber! I was so embarrassed and I can't believe that something like this could happen to me in such a nice hotel! By this time (practically 45 minutes after it happened!), Gwen and all her brothers came into my room and everyone knew what had happened. I have never been so mortified. I guess I'll laugh about it someday, maybe . . .

My Most Embarrassing Moment

Kevin:
  I hAve done Some very very
embARRAssing things fRom Scoring foR
the wRong teAm to sAying something
ReAlly stupid At the wRong time
in the wRong plAce. let's see, the
mAin thing I'm hARASSed foR is when
I fell All the wAy down fRom the
top bleAcheR At A volleybAll gAme
oh yeAh like 100 people sAw me
but thAnkfully I cAn lAugh About
it b/c I AlwAys scRew up And Am
clumsy.

Billy:
  When I dropped the football or puked on my
gram during Grandparent's Day.

Emma:
  The most embarrassing ever was one
day in class when I was talking about
this girl and her boyfriend and I like
screamed out in the room, "Oh yeah, I
hear they've been going for a yEAR and

My Most Embarrassing Moment

they haven't even hooked up yet!" But I
totally forgot that girl was In my class
and the whole class started laughing at me
for saying something STUPID with the
girl standing right there.

Baxter:

Almost half of what I do embarrasses me and
the worst part isn't even the fact that I'm
embarrassed, but the fact that I turn RED RED
RED!

Katie:

The most embarrassing moment ever
happened last spring at a Community Club
convention. I had to go up to receive this
prestigious award at the front of the
auditorium, but we were sitting in the back
row. As I walked down toward the stage,
cameras were fixed on me and the full
image of me climbing the stairs was
projected on 3 giant screens in front of
something like 1,000 people or more. I
was soooo humiliated!

My Most Embarrassing Moment

<u>Jake</u>:

    I fell once on the lacrosse field when I was going downfield. Like a million people saw me do it and were laughing. But we won anyway, I remember that.

<u>Marybeth</u>:

    I don't get embarrassed easy. Just can't think of anything. Hey—guess I'm 2 perfect!

<u>Teresa</u>:

    There's this one incident at the semiformal last year when I had on high-heeled shoes. I always wear them, but these particular shoes were slippery ones. So anyway I was walking across the empty dance floor to talk to my friends and a good song was on and I was singing and bouncing and suddenly my feet slipped out from under me and I fell on my ASS! The worst part of all was that this cute group of guys saw me do it!!

127

Billy

Being at parties and drinking w/my friends just makes me wish I had a girlfriend. I think about it a lot for some reason like why any of my relationships can't seem to fly and I don't fully get it. I thought the girls liked me, they always smile. Then again maybe it's just that "cute" thing. Now I realize that girls find me cute *BUT* I am never bf material. Katie said once I was friend material. That's what I've heard from others too. Do I sometimes come across badly? I think I'm a good guy, but maybe not everyone else does? I'm confused about this one.

Is it possible to be perfect b/c I mostly can't settle for anything less than that—I can't help it. Of course this means that I am disappointed a lot so I wanna understand how that happens. Does it happen b/c I have unrealistic standards like my bro/me? I was dreaming about a 1450 SAT score. Is that at all possible in the best of all possible worlds? Today I got up, listened to Howard Stern on the radio, and goofed around. Even though I want high scores, I am so lazy so I don't know how to get them. Sometimes I want everything to just come to me, I am tired of fighting for it. That includes girls.

Teresa

Dec 30 (5:45 p.m.)

I was so excited tonite because I saw this guy I have a crush on at Vincent's alumni hockey game! It was the annual alumni event that we always go to as a family, at least me, Vin, and my dad. The guy I have a crush on is called Hammy (his real name is Hamilton—isn't that cool?) and he is now 20 and goes to the University of Colorado and he says he's a huge ski bum and I think I could just die every time I see him around JFK over the holidays and stuff. He is so good-looking he would make snow melt! I am such a sap!

But seriously, I *DO* have a crush on him & always have and actually that's the sad part. Like he called our house a few times three or four days ago to talk to Vincent and then I answered and just started talking, talking, talking to Hammy before he could change the subject. I don't know if that's what he wanted, but I didn't care.

So tonite there he was again in all his glory and believe it or not he smiled right at me—I swear! We even talked once the game was over and we were talking about how I could drive with him in the car because he was 20. Then he asked for my *NUMBER*! I have the hugest crush now. I just hope he calls! I made my dad take a picture of us so I could keep it forever!! Jeez, I'm not a *little* boy crazy, am I? Why can't I find someone great? Will

129

Hammy *EVER* call me? Of course, the fact that he's going back to Colorado in a week is kind of a problem.

Marybeth

December 30th

Okay, some things take longer than others to get out of your system. Like Matt still has not called. And I still *DO NOT CARE*, but I can't help but notice the reality of the situation. Even though he's a jerk, he's glued inside my head.

Of course lucky me, Rick Wright called late tonite like @ midnight. He was shitfaced. What is the problem w/me and guys these days?

Going over to Emma's boyfriend Cliff's house tomorrow nite & that should be cool I guess. New Year's solo.

Emma

12/30, 7:45 PM

I have a *HUGE* problem. See, Marybeth really likes this guy Matt, and I really thought he liked her too. They hung out like twice and he used to talk to her on the phone all the time. Well, this other friend

130

of mine, Lance, he knows Matt too. So Lance called me up and he says that from the beginning he knew this whole relationship would be bad for Marybeth and that Matt would break her heart. And then he said that Matt didn't really like her anymore and he felt bad because he knew how much she liked him. I swore to Lance that I wouldn't say anything to Marybeth about those facts because he'd get in trouble with Matt, but now I just don't know. I don't want ANYONE to get in trouble or to get hurt.

But here's where the problem REALLY comes in. I'm supposed to head over to Cliff's with Marybeth for New Year's Eve and she just called to ask if maybe we could ask Matt to come too. So she wants to call him up. What am I supposed to tell her? I can't say sure because of what Lance said but I can't say no either because she would start to suspect something was up. I just feel that it's wrong not to tell her. She is my best friend.

I don't want to hurt her feelings by telling her, but I also can't stand around and watch Matt break her heart. That would be awful, especially since we're on vacation and it's almost New Year's Eve. What should I do? I guess I will wait a little while and see what happens. I mean, maybe it is better if she finds out on her own? I am soooooo confused. I just wish I could talk to someone about this like Baxter or someone.

Baxter

Tonight I had a *GREAT* time. Billy called me up and asked if I wanted to go to the movies and I said fine. Now that took a little convincing for my parents. I never had one of my friends drive me anywhere for the night, and since I am the youngest, my mom gets worried. So Mom and Dad asked if Billy was a good driver and I said yes of course, which he is. I just agreed that I would call them up as soon as I got to the mall. A lot of people were there and we got tickets and rushed in. The only bad part was these girls sitting behind us who would not *SHUT UP*. Afterward we went to the Silverado Diner. That brings my total visits there to 2. When I called my mom to tell her where we were, she was very pleased. She loved me for that later. I met my 11:00 curfew too. Billy's a good friend.

Billy

12-31
Bax is a good buddy. We caught a movie last night and had a few laughs. I like vacations since I spend more time with different friends, not always the same football crew. Bax is good because he likes my stupid

132

jokes and he was so psyched that we were driving alone when it was dark and night. I was too. It's so much freedom now to have a car. As long as Dad lets me continue to have the driving privileges, which he's been bad about in the past.

Today is the last day of the year and I can't believe it at all. So weird. And it's a Thursday, which just feels so ordinary, I don't know. Some of the guys from the team want me to go to this really big party tonight but I have to figure out how I'm gonna get there. I wanna drink so there's no way I'm gonna drive. I can't risk getting in any more trouble, plus that's too dangerous. When I'm out with my football friends it's beer, partying, and girls and nonstop fun fun fun. Parties w/them are just the greatest. We have beverages, of course, and drink the night away and basically go crazy. Not much talking just a lot of laughs. NOT horseplaying-wise like when we're on the bus, but more like yelling and dancing and stuff. When the action and beer disappear is when we finally start to calm down a little, like 4 or 5 A.M. Then we try to get our grooves on and usually try hooking up w/some girl who also got drunk. I have never done anything much though, just some kissing.

I know this one guy who is kind of an asshole who took advantage of this one girl from our grade and I think they had sex and he made her go down on him like in his car or something. I say that's so wrong. You can't be drunk. Both people should be equal or else something is really messed. Not like

I've been seeing any action lately so who am I to talk. Maybe this coming year will bring me more luck in that department. Lee says I should just worry about grades and sports and the rest will come along afterward. I hope he's right. Of course, he usually is.

Kevin

12/31

It's late Thursday and today we actually had a swim practice—well we have been having them all week. Today was the 15-layer strip down and me and Lazlo won the award for best dressed. See what happens is that you have to wear stuff and strip it off while you get into the water and swim a certain distance the fastest. So anyway, b/c the rest of the team calls us the Tom and Jerry swimmers (cause Mick is shorter than me and looks like a mouse I guess), we dressed like a cat and a mouse. It was awesome and soooo funny. It was really hard to swim w/all the clothes on at first but it got easier and later Coach Foster gave us OJ and doughnuts. He's a really nice guy. It was really nice of him.

Ok, now I was thinking today that now that it's gonna be a brand-new year like as of midnight tonight and I am finally and officially unattached, I just wanna know why Katie Holmes can't be my woman? I want that girl soooo freaking bad it isn't even funny. I would do *ANYTHING* to go out w/her. And maybe more. Hee hee hee. She is just *SO SO SO* gorgeous and I love her. I wanna marry her and have like 500 kids. We're probably total opposites but I don't even care I just love her! I don't get why people portray actors and actresses as imperfect b/c they so seem *PERFECT* to me. Like Jennifer Love Hewitt she doesn't seem to have anything wrong with her at all. Why them and not me? I sometimes wonder if maybe these people have like more spiritual or mental probs instead of physical ones b/c there's no way they're totally perfect it's impossible. Ok, maybe I'm just jealous in a way. I know I'm not freakin hot as hell or like to die for like them. I am like totally dysfunctional in comparison to JLH and the rest of them. Truth is I feel below average sometimes. I need to work my ass off to be even the littlest bit happy. I want something bigger, better, more that can make me happier and more content. And of course, my future lies in someone else's hands too. Hopefully that person is generous enough to give me what I want & to judge me for me and only me. Oh yeah and *I WANT IT ALL* by the way. Ta ta

Jake

December 31
Well, today is the last day of the year and I have gone through a lot w/my family and friends. I guess

it has been an ok year. I will miss some of the things.

I got off work today so I can go out tonight and play and party. Yesterday I got only one lead at Stewart Mortgage Co. and then after that I went to Jonny's to play cards. Me, Jonny, Mick Lazlo, and Jonny's brother Duke played. We got bored while we were playing so we started drinking. But it was ok— Jonny's parents were home. We were drinking beer. Jonny's brother Duke who's 21 got a case of Budweiser for Xmas as a joke. So we had some of that. It was kind of warm though. I won about $4 playing cards and the others won about the same but Lazlo lost almost $15. He's so bad and we tried to get him to stop playing but he wouldn't cut out. He even cashed in this Christmas gift, some mall gift certificate, so he could keep betting more. Later on after cards we watched The Playboy Channel. We always do that at Jonny's place.

I feel like all we are doing is spending money lately. Since my parents can't work it's like everything is disappearing fast. My mom wants to put a deck out back but doesn't know if she will be able to afford it. But that would be great because then Dad would have a ramp and be able to go outside more on his own. All this is why I need to work harder at my job. I have to try and help out and tell my mom to spend less on me and more on Dad and the house and everyone else. I want things to be right this year.

Katie

Happy New Year! Well, almost . . . Today was a crummy beach day. It was cloudy, but we still had some fun. Gwen and I spent the day at the beach and pool at the Moorings Club. We also played tennis over there. Despite the weather, we really had fun. I actually got more sunburned. I guess the sun is strong even when it's gray outside. Actually we spent a substantial amount of time inside these beach cabanas when it started raining. We played cards. Meanwhile everyone else left for the entire afternoon. Mom took Patti to the medical clinic up the road because Patti was feeling a little dizzy last night. She's okay though. I think she maybe needs to rest up a little bit. I don't think it's a relapse like over the summer. I hope not. Ever since Patti was diagnosed with this blood disorder things have been a little stressful for my parents.

New Year's Eve tonight will be spent at the club with Gramps and Gram. They're planning fireworks and there's going to be dancing. Dad says he thinks we should celebrate in a BIG way! Maybe it will be a dinner with family and friends, and it might be a much older and rather "stiff" crowd, but I'm sure we can liven it up! Gram says she expects us all to dress up like little princesses. She is so adorable! The only unfortunate part about the whole evening will be being apart from Brad. I wish I could be with Brad on New Year's Eve. This afternoon when a bunch of random guys tried to pick us up on the beach, all I could think about was Brad. Gwen was joking about letting the guys take us out for drinks so we'd have someone to kiss at midnight! But I wish *Brad* was here for me to kiss. I suppose we'll just have to make up for it a few days late. I'm just about at the point where I can't bear not seeing him for any longer. There's nothing I can do, though, but keep remembering that we'll be together again in three days.

I keep thinking about how the coming year is going to be a big year in my life, maybe the biggest ever. It will bring my driver's license, senior year, hopefully college acceptance to Stanford. Every year I compose an endless list of New Year's resolutions. This year I am hoping mostly to be healthy and happier than ever. Nothing more. Well, losing 10 pounds would be nice I guess, even though Gwen says I'm already skinny enough. I need to fit into my teeny costume in *The Boy Friend* when I go back to school. But I won't push it. I just feel like I need to do everything and anything I can to make sure to keep myself, my family, Brad, and my other friends happy and healthy. If I can succeed in doing that I will be prosperous and successful.

New Year's Resolutions

Marybeth:

1. Lose 2 lbs. every month

2. Go to bed earlier so I'm not so damn tired every day!

3. Change the way I spend time like getting a JOB (I'm applying to the drugstore up the street) so I can be more independent w/spending and stuff. I don't feel like grubbing off my parents anymore. . . .

4. Get my tongue pierced (Mom and Dad still say no but I hope this year I can) & change other things about my look like maybe I should wear some more makeup other than mascara but these prob. won't happen

5. Deal w/ my brother Mitch

Billy:

Get smart about schoolwork—better grades or else!

Keep driving—without getting any more tickets!

Stay in better touch with Lee at college—get into U Michigan too!

New Year's Resolutions

<u>Emma:</u>

1. Change my relationship w/my dad. I think I have hurt his feelings sometimes by mouthing off and I don't want to do that anymore because I am lucky to have a father at all and I should appreciate it.

2. Be my own person more and don't let others influence me so much. I think I need to be a little meaner so people don't walk all over me.

That's all I can think of except getting better grades too.

<u>Kevin:</u>

GonnA woRK My ASS off to get whAt I cAn to mAke me hAppy!!!

<u>Katie:</u>

1. Get more organized and reduce my stress load!!!

2. Get elected to the Intrastate Committee and obviously get into a good college and do very well on my AP exams.

New Year's Resolutions

3. Actually have a boyfriend for the new year! (I have always been so cursed in this area! But now that Brad's in my life . .)

Jake:

Study stuff for college + start learning about business because I want to major in business management
Spend even more time with my dad
Make more $$$
Find a cute girl

Baxter:

1. Do better in PHYSICS!!
2. Drive well so my mom is happy and lets me go out more at night
3. Maybe drop out of Community Club
4. Go out with Megan finally
5. Focus on my grades and classes because this year decides my entire future!

New Year's Resolutions

Teresa:

1. Change how I relate to people
and not seclude myself into one
little group when I want to hang
out with EVERYONE.

2. Make over my soul and become
more spiritual-like, but also try
out some new hairstyles and
makeup and losing a few pounds
wouldn't hurt either. I've never
been on a diet before, but I want
to cut back on all of the junk
food I eat and focus on eating
healthy foods for once.

3. Get A's in every subject at
least once this year!

4. Attempt being in a good mood
every day in school. I know there
are going to be days where I
just want to go home and be
alone, but I shouldn't take it out
on my friends and other people.

5. Work on not letting people get
to me as much and avoid being
walked on.

Teresa

Dear Diary,

It's the *NEW YEAR*! Yay! My New Year's Eve was wonderful. And before that even happened—during the day—Hammy called me! I am soooooo happy right now. We talked and it was really cool. And that nite I went to Wendy's house. She was having a BYOA party (as in Bring Your Own Alcohol). I managed to sneak some vodka and beer plus the rules to this awesome drinking game. So I went to Wendy's and ended up getting pretty drunk. I really don't remember too much to be honest. I do remember our friend Gina puking almost the entire night, which was gross. And during the nite at some point Hammy beeped me! So I called him back and he asked me to go to his friend's house but I couldn't because I had no ride. I was mad about not being able to go, but it was better to stay at Wendy's. I wouldn't have dissed my friends on New Year's Eve!

The one thing I *DEFINITELY* do remember is crying when the ball dropped in Time's Square. We were watching it on the TV. I know why I got upset too, apart from the drinking. I had been having *SUCH* a bad year, I can't fully explain how relieved I was to feel that it had finally ended for real. It was so bad and when it wasn't bad—it was *BORING*. I am so sick of this guy business and I realize now that I hate Zach for dicking me around and I just don't wanna deal with any crap in the coming year. I gladly kiss last year goodbye. Time to start anew!

marybeth

Cliff's New Year's party was ok. I played Sony PlayStation most of the nite b/c I was liking that. And he did have 40 oz. so I was drinking all nite. That was great but today I woke up feeling wicked bloated & determined to lose weight and start the new year in a positive way—even though Matt is still blowing me off.

Another reason New Year's was weird actually b/c of all people I got an e-mail wishing me Happy New Year from that kid Rick Wright. I checked online late last nite (well, this A.M. actually) after I got in. After everything that happened w/me and Rick, he still writes to me. He said he was sorry for calling me when he was drunk the other nite and wanted me to still be his friend. He actually said that he didn't want me to think he was some kind of stalker, which I don't of course, but I do wish he would just relax sometimes. Anyway, he ended by asking me to call him and saying I was a sweetheart. That was pretty nice I guess. Later on we talked online a little but it didn't mean much at all. He was telling me what parties he went to and all that. He was just sitting at home listening to the Stones. He loves them. Oh, maybe I'm wrong but even if he's being *SUPER* nice, I'm not gonna go there b/c I've been down this road w/Rick B4 and I really don't want to go thru it all again.

I think I need to go run or something. I'm gonna go call Baxter and see if he wants to run the reservoir w/me (like 3 miles around, almost a 5K). I dunno if he can make it, but I think he'll try.

Baxter

HAPPY HAPPY HAPPY NEW YEAR'S!

What a day!!!! It started out so funny. Marybeth called me and asked me for a favor. I said what? She asked if I would run with her. First I laughed really hard. Why did she call me—the most out of shape person—to run? But I said ok. We ran around the whole reservoir or at least 2 or 3 miles of it. It was fun actually and we lucked out and got a ride home.

Last night my whole family came over for dinner and it was a lot of fun. At like 9:30 I went over to this party at this guy Ron's house. When I got there everybody was already drunk. People are really funny when they're drunk. I think maybe I was the only person there who wasn't drinking but that didn't matter. I still had a total blast. Billy and this other guy Ron whose party it was tried to get me to have a drink but they gave up on me. Crazy stuff was happening. I left around 2 A.M.

p.s. Oh yeah, I almost forgot! While I was running today with Marybeth, I got a call from Megan. I couldn't believe that I missed it. I was a little bit pissed off. Then I beeped her around 2:30 and waited. I figured there was no way she would call me back . . . but *SHE DID*! We talked for an hour and a half.

I HER!

Billy

1-1

How cool is it that the New Year is here! Last nite was a total pisser going to this guy Ron's for drinks and partying until the wee hours. Bax showed up and wimped out of the whole festivities but claims he had a good time. I guess that's possible, but I was too busy mostly to notice. I was also afraid that Blair D. would be there b/c apparently Ron is seeing her now. I can't keep track. Everyone

ends up seeing everyone else I swear. I'm glad that I
am single right now so I don't have to worry about
someone else.

Emma

Happy New Year! I can't believe it. It really doesn't
feel like a new year to me. It really doesn't feel like
Christmas or Hanukkah or anything else either.
Junior year is going by so quickly.

Guess what? Sherelle thought I was mad at her for
some reason. Well, I think she thought that because
the other night I didn't talk to her that much.
Whatever. She knows I wasn't really talking with anyone except for Cliff so what is wrong? She told
Marybeth too that I was mad at her and then said that
she didn't really care anymore about my "attitude."
Gimme a break! The only reason she hung out w/us
AT ALL was because Bobby was out of town. If he had
been home she never would have gone out with us.
And no one will dare say that to her face. Maybe
someone should. It just really bothers me that we are
only good enough company when someone else is
gone. That's not fair to us. But who cares anymore,
right? Not me! Anyway, last nite I decided that I
would be a wiseass to her, just to see what was up, if
she really was as mad as she said. So I called up to

ask her point-blank what are you doing, Sher? And she said she didn't know, which was a definite lie since I knew from Marybeth that she was going to her cousin's place. Okay, then she said let's talk later on to see what's up and I said ok, I'll call you back. So like 5 seconds later Cliff calls, I make plans with him, and never call Sherelle back. So I guess what happened too is that Marybeth never called her back either. And the two of us went to Cliff's place. Okay. So then Marybeth called Sher from Cliff's house and left a message on her machine kind of like, "What is your problem?" It was pretty obnoxious. Apparently Sher called Marybeth back at like 1 A.M. and woke MB up. Sher was *PISSED*! Marybeth just ignored her and fell back asleep.

Cliff's—apart from the Sherelle incident—was a good time. When we first got there we were just chilling out in his room watching a skate video and playing video games. It was fun. Then his brother left and went to get alcohol. At like 10:15 we started to drink. Then the night became really good. I think I was as drunk as the last time I drank when my cousin bailed me out and I ran into Sherelle at the Silverado. Cliff was worse than me. Marybeth was only a little buzzed. Cliff and I were just laughing a lot and lying there on the bed laughing some more. He was so funny he was like, this is my girlfriend Emma West. I'd like you to meet my girlfriend Emma. I have never seen him act that way before. Then he was saying that he loved me and how much he meant it and wasn't just saying it because he was drunk. No, he really meant it. I was like ok. Whatever you say. Whatever. And the whole time his mom and dad were right downstairs. In fact, his mom made us nachos to eat they were so *HOT*! Really yummy. I wonder how Cliff's parents don't know what we're doing upstairs? They're always home when we drink. Maybe they think it's better because at least we're not driving and we're home safe. I don't know why. But all in all, a good New Year's Eve!

xoxoxoxxo

p.s. When I finally came home there was this mean e-mail from Sher on my computer with her claiming that she kept beeping us all night and we ignored her but that it wasn't a big deal and why was I making it into one? But I answered back and told her that the whole thing was pretty stupid and that she could be mad about shit if she wanted but I was *TOTALLY* over it all. And by the way—she *never* beeped me.

Jake

January 1

It feels weird to write in my journal on the first day of the new year. I guess I'll get used to it. Last night was fun. After dinner with my parents my mom didn't want me to go out anywhere but I convinced her to let me. I just had to promise to be back home before the ball dropped. So I went over to Kevin's and we played Nintendo 64 again just like the other night. We couldn't drink. But later everyone came back home with me and I drank almost an entire bottle of champagne with my mom right there. She didn't even notice. We went outside and lit a few fireworks and then everyone went home.

Kevin

1/1

Yesterday was really slackish except for the New Year's part & today is like crap cuz I am wasted & thank goodness my mom let me sleep in today though until like 2:30 in the afternoon. I think she knows I wasn't home last nite until after 2 so she's being sweet. I just lazed around all day like a load and can't get up enuf energy to do very much at all. So last nite my family went out for New Year's Eve dinner and after it was hard figuring out what else I wanted to do b/c I didn't want to drive and I wanted to get drunk but no one else wanted to and I called *EVERYONE*. I was really really pissed off that no one else wanted to drink on the one night when I actually could, so me and some other friends and Jake just chilled here at my place. Oh yeah, Cristina was supposed to be around but she was a no-show I don't know what happened. The high point of the night was lighting these fireworks like sparklers that we found in the basement so that was cool. But it was kind of still a bad way for me to start the new year b/c again I am left not getting to do what I wanna do, which is drink, and of course I guarantee in like 2 days from now these same friends will be shitty to me and then that's supposed to be A-OK w/me. Ohhhh well. Ta ta I'm gone.

p.s. One more thing wait about tonite late I went online for a while and talked w/Sherelle. That's been a long time for me. She's been hanging w/a new crowd not like old times when we would see each other a lot. Me and Marybeth were just talking about how much we notice Sherelle has changed. She's different now that she's been w/Bobby. It's kinda his fault. I think maybe b/c he's away w/his family this week is why all of a sudden she's getting friendlier w/some of us again. But that's bullshit b/c I bet the minute he's back she'll be busy all over again. All that's happening is that she's saying to herself, Okay, now that my boyfriend's gone I'd better find some new people to hang with. I guess maybe I don't *really* care, not as much as some other people like MB and Emma do, but I sometimes wonder if when her relationship w/Bobby is over, then *WHAT'S GONNA HAPPEN*?!! Junior year has put this weird curse on some friendships this year like they are changing so much I don't get it ok ta ta for real now.

Katie

Well, it's a brand-new year but nothing much has changed for me. I'm still in Florida and loving every minute of it. But I do need to get home. I miss Brad most of all! So let me recap what happened last night. I was tired and went back early from partying but everyone else stayed out until after 4 A.M.! We had dinner around 9 o'clock and actually stayed at the club for a little over 3 hours. They had noisemakers and a huge spread and a band with dancing and tons of people! There was confetti everywhere on the tables and floor. What a celebration! Our party took up the whole back of the restaurant and everyone was hyper—especially the parents. I thought it was great to spend New Year's with so many family members and friends— something I know I probably wouldn't have done if I had been home. I'm sure most of my friends went drinking. When we left, the "kids" went back to the Driftwood resort to change into comfy clothes and that gave me a minute to call Brad. He made me feel so bad for not being with him! I wish I could have been, but I really thought it was more important to let him be with his friends. I promised him that we'd spend next New Year's Eve together for sure. I hope so.

When the group of us went out again *without* the

parents we went to this bar/restaurant right on the water that has dancing under the moonlight. It was *PACKED* with people a lot of whom were our age, or at least over 21. They didn't card me or Gwen so we could do whatever we wanted. I got hit on by at least 6 different men, which I could not believe happened, but of course I blew them all off. I have my Brad! Gwen was laughing about it though because it was like I was a magnet or something for all these guys. She said I was her "bait." Some of the attempts were humorous though.

1. This really hideous guy who was maybe 24 grabbed my shoulder and asked me to dance and then asked me do I want a drink with him. I smile and walk away.

2. This *OLD* guy, maybe 60 or so, grabbed my arm and asked me if I wanted to meet his son who was 23 or something. Gwen actually thought the son was cute but I was not interested. I walk away.

3. This guy walked up to me and Gwen both and asks if we're from Sweden. I guess he was because when we shook our heads, *HE* walked away!

4. These 3 different, pretty normal-looking guys came over to me and said how exotic and beautiful I am. I just laugh politely and walk away over toward where Gwen is.

5. The same 3 guys followed me over to Gwen and told me again that I am so pretty and do we want to dance with them? I shake my head no. Total dorks.

After that last incident, I told Gwen I wanted to

leave. I had enough! I couldn't take it anymore. I missed Brad so much and I just wanted to crawl into my bed and sleep.

Marybeth

My neck hurt all day today. And then I burnt my tongue on a cup of hazelnut latte coffee and it totally sucks b/c it is killing me! What's with all this pain? I can't stand it.

I asked my dad if he would show me how to drive stick and he said he would but he doesn't have any time to do it. I also asked Mom if I could go snowboarding tomorrow. She didn't give me an answer yet though. It's supposed to rain but I hope it doesn't.

p.s. Oh yeah, apparently Sherelle and Emma are still fighting.

p.p.s. I am bored. Here's part of an e-mail from me and Kevin. We just got off the computer.

Mrbiggie417:	hey hunny whassup
2much4u2:	*not much what r u up 2?*
Mrbiggie417:	tired
2much4u2:	*hate that but I have the opposite insomnia*
Mrbiggie417:	I know I get that sometimes like I think I've been sleeping some long ass time and then I wake up and it's

154

	only been like an hour
2much4u2:	*yeah*
Mrbiggie417:	wanna do something later
2much4u2:	*I wanna go running I think but it's cold outside*
Mrbiggie417:	yeah no shit LOL
2much4u2:	*ha ha captain obvious but seriously I do wanna go*
Mrbiggie417:	you know I have been thinking about taking kick boxing
2much4u2:	*yeah whatever kev*
Mrbiggie417:	no really I think they have lessons at the Y or something
2much4u2:	*what r u gonna do, kick my ass? Ha ha j/k*
Mrbiggie417:	yeah basically my little hoochina, I could do that couldn't I?
2much4u2:	*ha ha you're a laugh riot jeez louise*
Mrbiggie417:	ok u know what I gotta run
2much4u2:	*no I wanted to run*
Mrbiggie417:	yeah I get it I should call you runningmama online
2much4u2:	*that's not funny*
Mrbiggie417:	ok how about jugs38ddd?
2much4u2:	*LOL but that's not my size stupid*
Mrbiggie417:	yeah but if you went online to chat everyone would wanna cyber sex w/ you
2much4u2:	*then definitely not ok*
Mrbiggie417:	sorry MB I gotta leave for real now so buhbye
2much4u2:	*bye you*

Teresa

Dear Diary,

Well, the exciting news is that Hammy and I have been corresponding on e-mail and over the phone, which is excellent! I love him so much and hope that something interesting comes out of this, please!

I talked to a lot of different people and it seems like no one really did anything too exciting over New Year's. That shocked me (and of course it shocked my mom, who thinks we should all be out having fun all the time J/K) but oh well. I wish that this club still was around in town. They had these teen nites once a month and I miss the fun atmosphere—a couple of hundred teens dancing and having a good time, absorbing the rhythm of the music so I could lose myself in it. If we had a no-school Monday, they'd have parties on Sundays even. And it was the BEST place to meet guys.

So in honor of the new year, I looked up my forecast in this horoscope book and this is what they had for Libra for the new year:

Motto:	I Communicate	← *Last year's was I Connect*
Ruling Planet:	Venus	
Colors:	Rose, blue	
Gems:	Jade, sapphire	
Body Parts:	Lower back, hands	*Just like my b-day party!!*
Element:	Air	

Quality: Cardinal

This means I like to start new things ←

Flowers: Roses, blue irises, daisies

Oh and also, the intro to my sign for the new year says that I am a born communicator. That's good, right? And also there's this part about how my planet is Venus, which is planet *Love*, and that guys adore my femininity. Wow. Now if only that stuff were true ha ha. Joke's on me. Lookin' for love in all the wrong places!

Emma

1/3, 8:05 PM

I think Sherelle is so *WRONG* for writing me that nasty e-mail the other day. I am still steaming about that one. Ok maybe it was only partly nasty, but still I am sick of these lame e-mails she sends me saying how we never do anything together and why am I still so mad at her? Whatever. It's what she does every time I can see it coming.

There is so much more I could say about Sher but I won't because it just will make things worse. I could have brought up bad details about her relationship w/Bobby like how she is so exclusive to him and his

157

friends. It seems like we are in a fight all the time about this stuff. And the worst part is that she denies it all and has no idea how many people see her having this total change and talking shit about who she is. She just has not realized and thinks she is too good for everyone else a little bit. I heard from MB that Jake sent her this terrifying e-mail that basically ripped her to shreds. It said that she was a big faker. I can't believe he had the nerve to do that. Jake is fearless.

Jake

January 3

I worked on the snowblower today even though we had no snow. Yesterday was a great day. I woke up and had a good breakfast and grabbed a few guys from the neighborhood. We were going to go ice skating at the reservoir because it was completely frozen—even though skating there is supposedly against the law.

Anyway, while we were sort of skating an ambulance saw us and called in the emergency. We were breaking the law. So we skated back to where we started and were actually caught by the cops. All we had to do was give him our names and we were told we could under no circumstances skate there. So we left and went back toward home to skate in the pond behind my parents' place instead. But only part of it was frozen so we ruined our skates by having to walk on rocks to get back.

Then the worst part happened. I was just next to the golf course and I fell in knee deep like up to my knees in shallow water and ice and nasty-smelling mud and all of a sudden I realized how we were totally lost. Someone else tried to stand on a less mushy part and fell into the ice too. My friend had to get one of those giant sticks that you use when you hike or to just keep your balance. It was wild. One of the guys started taking pictures and we were laughing and falling into the mud a lot more. Someone told me to strip down to my boxers because my pants were totally scraping against my legs it was so so so gross and my thigh was rubbed red. Eventually we took off the skates and went home though, thank goodness, and we had to hurry because we were going out to eat. Dinner was Kev, Mick Lazlo, Marybeth, and lots of other people, including this chick Diane Russo again. Oh yeah, I wanted to hook up w/her so much but I didn't.

p.s. Again I could have tried a few more times too but I just didn't do it ha ha.

Kevin

It's late on Sunday nite the very last day of winter vacation and tomorrow we are back at school! So tonite I am making sure I'm all set to go w/my clothes and all that. I have just come off of one of the worst days ever yesterday even though dinner started out fun w/me, Jake, Micky Lazlo, Marybeth, and Diane. It was the after-dinner part that got weird and I cannot believe what happened there as we all left to go to Lazlo's house b/c no one expected any of this. Meanwhile at Lazlo's who should come over too but Cristina and May and ok first of all they all drank, which was bad. I mean, a few of them (including Marybeth) didn't drink right away, they talked and laughed. Not me. For me, it was like the whole environment put me in a pissy bad mood. I was *PISSED OFF* and it was like *NOT* the time *at all* to ask me to be the designated driver. But leave it to Cristina, she kept asking me to drive. And Marybeth and Lazlo knew I couldn't deal with her and take everyone in my wheels. They could just tell.

Ok, so what happens next is that instead of exploding and telling them to fuck off I just say fine get into the car I will drive you. And that's what gets me, being used just for my license. I know they're friends and all, but still I bet they would never let themselves get pissed off enough if it wasn't something for their benefit. I mean when Cristina *knows* I am pissy and in a bad mood, don't be so selfish that you can only have things *YOUR* way. That sucks. I don't know how else to explain the event in more detail except that I felt *REALLY* used and shit. To me life is like this crock of shit that you mainly have to deal with. Yeah, we all make these choices in life but most of it will suck regardless. I can understand why people drink and do drugs and keep lying to themselves and think that will make everything better, but it won't. I am just so sick of all this stress around me. Driving can *REALLY BE A PAIN*.

p.s. By the way, school is confirmed to start *TO-MORROW* very early so rise and shine.

p.p.s. Am I selfish just b/c I was mad about driving people to their homes? All I wanted was someone to say something to me about appreciating the ride but everyone was too busy off in like their own little wonderland.

Marybeth

January 3rd

Last nite I went to eat w/Kevin, Jake, Mick, Diane, and this other girl I only met once. We went out for Indian food and after that picked up Jonny + Cristina who joined us at Mick's place where we played some pool and stuff. Kev got a little hot under the collar about the driving, but I think he's ok now. I couldn't believe he was so mad for like no reason at all.

p.s. No snowboarding b/c of the rain.

January 3

I hung out with Billy last nite and for no acceptable reason he called me selfish. But he wouldn't tell me why. I had so much homework over this break and I got none done over vacation. I had to read all of *Huckleberry Finn,* 2 chapters for chem, and naturally, for physics I had to do problems. I also did one extra-credit assignment for math just to cover all my bases. It's been a looooong day and now school starts again tomorrow. Yeeps! This *SUCKS*.

Homework Homework

Baxter:

I study at my desk alone in my room but sometimes I call people up and we quiz each other back and forth.

Emma:

Sometimes when I have a major test my stomach gets all jumpy with nerves but that usually goes away. Mostly I get quizzed by friends like Baxter and that really helps me, but I can't spend too much time with people because then we start talking and not working.

Katie:

I comprehend most things in class so when I have to repeat 30 problems at night, it feels like a ponderous task. I study alone when I do study, in my office. And I realize now that one test does not necessarily mean anything in the long run, with the exception of the SAT.

Homework

Homework

Homework

Homework

Jake:

I never study except for vocabulary and I don't carry anything to feel lucky in a test, not even a rabbit's foot.

Marybeth:

I never get bugged out by tests and I study alone when I study, but all I really do is read and reread my notes 1 or 2 times—with the radio or TV on b/c there's no way I can concentrate in total silence.

Kevin:

We don't have any study hall so I have to study mostly at home for tests and exams and other homework. Here's what I do. I have this Buddha that when you rub its tummy it brings you good luck and I have brought it to _every_ exam since freshman year b/c it just works 4 me.

Homework Homework

<u>Teresa</u>:

When I was younger like in middle school and even in the beginning of high school, I was always studying, highlighting my notes, or something. But it <u>always</u> paid off and somewhere between then and now I stopped caring so much about studying.

<u>Billy</u>:

Schoolwork is easier to do when you're alone, but I like to call Bax for homework help. He's such a brainiac.

Billy

1-4

I don't get Bax. Take last night for example. I really thought the guy could take a joke. I mean I was only kidding around with him on the phone when all of a sudden his line went blank. He hung up on me? I thought it was an accident but it was more than that. He's never done anything like that before. Maybe it was a mistake. Maybe not. I don't know for sure. I haven't seen him yet today. Anyway, I'm thinking about maybe joining the school newspaper and I know he's on it so I thought maybe he could help me decide what to do. I think I'd better start adding on some more versatile extra-curricular activities into my course load. Before we know it, college visits are going to be here, and then college applications, which are awful. I remember when Lee went through all that. He bit all his nails off.

Katie

January 5
@ 4:13 P.M.

Got back from Florida two days ago! The weather there was perfect. In fact, the whole vacation was perfect, *BUT* I have spent the last 24 hours picking myself up because I had a little temporary breakdown yesterday (Monday). I was so overwhelmed with everything when I got back to school that I called up Brad on Monday night crying. I was a mess. I picked myself up and reassembled though and spent the whole evening trying to reorganize my life and then I even stayed up until 1am doing work. Maybe it's not good to stay up without sleep—but I have to learn how to function like that! I have to be okay!

Winter is *ALWAYS* nuts for me because of the musical—I love my part! It makes me think about what part of me likes acting and performing. All my life I think I have been most drawn to two different career aspirations, neither of which involves performance. Well, not really. I think I want to go into business or medicine. I have a passion for science and 2 summers ago I even had the chance to dissect a cadaver with my class at summer school. But I think sometimes that I don't want science because of the other people in those disciplines. I can't say I would want to spend 4 years with any of them since they are so, well, "dry." But I am also very good w/ideas and leadership so I have been leaning toward an interest more in business lately. We'll see what happens.

Tonight we had Community Club elections and they were so nerve-racking. Basically, what I had to do was put on a suit, do a 3-minute speech, and answer questions about absolutely anything at all. This was in a room filled with very important people. Lucky for me, however, my opponents dropped out right before they were supposed to go on and I *WON!*

So now I am officially a National Community Club Adviser for our region. I have been waiting for this since I was a freshman. I knew I could do it! It feels so good to know that my goal has been reached over the course of three years—I cannot even describe it! It is a big goal to have achieved too.

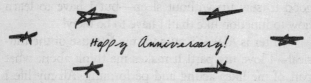

Happy Anniversary!

Tomorrow makes 4 whole months for me & Brad! We have to see each other but I have musical rehearsal and he has basketball practice, so I don't know when we'll do that exactly. I did tell him NO *ROSES* though and he got embarrassed. I don't want him to feel like he has to get me something every single month. He's so sweet. He brought me something else! He got the CD for *Lion King* and I feel like all the songs are exactly perfect for describing how I feel sometimes lately. I'm trying so hard and just hoping, hoping that I will succeed. Brad knew I had been feeling extra stressed and so he thought the sound track would inspire me. It did.

Jake

School is back and not inspiring me one little bit. I wake up, go to school, do my work, leave, go to work, come home around 9:30, do my homework, and watch TV: *Seinfeld* and *Friends* in reruns. *EVERY DAY* the same thing.

Tonight I got four leads at work though so maybe I will make some cash for myself and some for helping my mom out. She said I shouldn't worry about her but I am. I'm also gonna get it together w/Kevin and we're gonna snowblow some driveways in the neighborhood for cash.

It's snowing a lot right now and it's really cold. I'm cold.

Kevin

1/6

Like it is soooo cool outside white and shit and Jake & I are *SO PSYCHED* b/c we wanna make some mucho dinero snowblowing driveways in the area for cheap. Katie's dad even asked us if we wanted to come by them and do theirs. Yesssss!

Well, right now I am really really soooo tired there is just way too much happening and even tho it's like same shit different day, still I am feelin ok. The lady who is so dope who teaches life guarding she bought us all pizza today and that's about it though there are no real highlights to the day other than that one. Oh well, my swim coach put me in a bunch of races and that got me pretty wiped and oh yeah, went online had a fun convo w/MB late tonite B4 she went to bed. She & I have been hanging together more lately. Ok, so here's what we said.

2much4u2:	*hullo sweetie*
Mrbiggie417:	I am bored and tired but I don feel like goin to bed
2much4u2:	*yeah I feel exact the same*
Mrbiggie417:	you said in skool u been thinkin about a lotta shit, anything in particular?
2much4u2:	*sorta . . . well, Matt*
Mrbiggie417:	who? I am drawing a blank who is he
2much4u2:	*he's a senior and I like him but he is blowing me off*
2much4u2:	*yeah I feel pretty ditched*
Mrbiggie417:	yeah but I know what u mean been there
2much4u2:	*well that wuz buggin me this wk but then like that whole thing w/Sherelle I woke up suddenly and saw what it was for real*
Mrbiggie417:	yeah
2much4u2:	*I'm so glad we r close again*
Mrbiggie417:	me 2 yeah
2much4u2:	*you r like one of my best friends do u know that we can totally relate*

170

Mrbiggie417:	I like these <3 to <3 convos w/u 2
2much4u2:	*same wavelength unlike some others*
Mrbiggie417:	ditto to you babe
2much4u2:	*I'm tired*
Mrbiggie417:	y don't you go 2 sleep and we'll deal w/Matt and the confusion L8er
2much4u2:	*ok*
Mrbiggie417:	luv ya don't worry
2much4u2:	*love u buddy <3 <3 <3*

Marybeth

January 6th

Boy do I wish it were still vacation! This week is turning out to be so weird. I've been talking to peeps I haven't heard from since the beginning of school . . . like GREG?! Weird. We talked 4ever. And I also talked to this other guy Big Paulie who I hooked up w/once—and he is soooo hot. Maybe we will hang out again. I dunno. Paulie called me up yesterday nite and we talked. Actually he woke me up b/c it was like midnight.

Tonite I was a basketball ref w/my bro Mitch. We're talking again BTW (by the way). Anyway, I can't stay mad 4ever. I have bigger things to worry about. I wanna guy who's mine I guess. And some other stuff too. I wanted so many things to happen this year and now it's going by so fast it's weird. Good night! I need my sleep ZzZzZzZ . . . .

Teresa

Jan 6 (1:30 p.m.)

Dear Diary,

I am totally upset. My brother Vincent's ex-gf Tara said she would get me a job at this babysitting service where she works. She is *always* going on about the kids and how much she loves it there and all that and how she makes $$ and has fun at the same time. Anyway, about a month ago when she told me she would be talking to her boss, I got so excited. I wanted a job there too!!!

But obviously, I assume they found someone else to work there because she never called me and she hasn't told me anything.

I REALLY NEED A JOB! Now that the new year is here, I have to start making money. I'm not in the spring musical (I think it's *The Boy Friend* and I wasn't into that) and they canceled the spring drama production, so I *do* have lots of free time. Last year when I did the play I had to quit my job (I was working in a health food store!). Anyway, I want a job now because I can start and work all the way thru the summer, which is sooooo cool!

Last year, my boss at the health food store used to make me so nervous all the time and I was never properly trained. He would always be on the phone and just leave me there to deal with all the problems. And people would come in and ask all sorts of complicated questions about wheat grass and vitamins and what on earth do I know about all that?! And not only that but he would leave me with all of the *RUDE* customers who I thought would be all mellow but who were really demanding!! And then I even had all the cleaning to do—all by myself too! I wanted to curse him out under my breath like *ALL THE TIME*. I had to quit. My body couldn't handle all the anxiety that's for sure.

Anyway, I need to find this new job and really important is that it should be in walking distance for me. Because both of my parents work, no one can ever take me anywhere and I am still the baby (no license) so I can't get around. That really limits my options. Oh well, I hope this year is better than last!

Baxter

January 6

This is the worst day and it's only the beginning of the year. This is *NOT* a good sign for the rest of time. Okay, first of all I failed my physics test. In fact, I only got one right out of 6 questions. Bad news but the truth is that he tested us on stuff we *HADN'T READ OR WORKED ON YET*!!!!

173

Okay, then I sucked in chem because Mr. MacTaggart gave us like 30 molecules that we had to learn in only 1 night, which is like the joke of all time. How is that possible? Doesn't he know that is impossible? I can't remember those!

Okay, then Megan hasn't called. Not even once.

Nothing is going right. How could I have been so wrong about my luck changing? Maybe tomorrow will be better. For now I'm just gonna stay inside and hang out w/Coconut. She's a good dog.

Emma

1/6, 10:35 PM

It is now after 10 and I just got off the phone with Baxter who says he is a little bored or upset or something. I don't know why he worries all the time about everything. He's already convinced that this year is going to be bad. Whatever.

I also talked earlier to Cliff and we are kind of fighting now but it's about really stupid shit. I don't know why. We had tried to make plans but his hours on his job really suck and we can't seem to find times that work for both of us. I mean, we will always have Sundays, but I want to see him during the week sometimes too. Oh well. I dunno. I mean he says maybe he'll change his schedule. Just wait and see is what he says and tells me I'm getting all worked up about nothing. But doesn't he understand like I don't see him all day at school because he's at Joyce and I'm at JFK and I just want to *SEE HIM*! I like being around him so much.

There are a lot of things that are different now than they were 3 months or so ago. Last fall it was not such a big deal ya know wow I'm starting my junior year of high school and I didn't think twice about college or about the fact that maybe friendships would be different or that I would be with someone like Cliff. But now as the year is moving on I am starting to think about this stuff a lot more. I am starting to realize that life is just moving fast and I have to try to catch up to it or I'm gonna like miss it. I hope this spring I can get it together. I hope I can see more of Marybeth and all my friends and that I won't feel so lonely anymore. That's the worst part. How can I fix that part?

Billy

1-6

Now that my brother Lee went back to U Michigan, the house is lonelier. I'm alone and school is back. Thought of calling Baxter but I don't think I will. I don't feel like playing video games. Shit. What should I do? I'd call Benjamin or Deke or one of the other guys from the football team, but I'm not into drinking or anything right now. Once again I find myself wishing I had a girlfriend. I have such mixed feelings about almost everything. I want something and then all of a sudden I don't want anything.

Jake

January 6

The snow has stopped, finally. Kevin and I made some serious cash with the snowblower last week. Tonight I have a shitload of homework already—I can't believe it.

My dad is feeling a little better. He said that the holidays made him feel a little more sad than ever before. He was worried that he was ruining it for all of us, which is not true. I'm always busy and worrying about him. Everyone at school knows he's real sick. No one asks me much about it, not even Katie or Baxter. But they do stuff for me like throwing me that birthday party in the fall and other stuff. And Kevin is always here like a brother. It's like when things get bad you really know who your friends are.

The only bad part is that now that we're all juniors we have all these other responsibilities and that makes us change. You can't just hang out all the time like we used to. We mostly just go to parties on weekends and drink or whatever. Now that we're all 16 and 17 most of us have to work after school or on weekends because we need to buy shit. I hope it snows more this weekend so I can make some easy money.

I try not to think too hard about what's happening next. If I think too much into the future, I get pissed. I start thinking is there any chance I will ever get a girl for Valentine's Day and will my dad ever get better this year? And what's going to happen to me and my friends? People suck if they are only obsessing right now about SATs. I know that matters but not so much. Time is running out—like someone could take your life away like that. Like my cousin Frankie. And that kid who went into his school and shot up his class. Those kids were the same as me. I have to keep doing as much as I possibly can right now. We all do.

Check out this sneak preview from

Teen.

real teens

Diary of a
Junior Year

volume 4

Marybeth

January 29th

Tonite I hung out w/a buncha friends including TJ! We didn't hook up or anything, but we had fun. I was like teasing TJ saying hey like when r we gonna hook ↑ but I was joking. He was like don't worry, MB, we will. It was cute!

But I think he's putting me on. It's kinda funny how we r when we're together. Oh well what can u do, right? Other than that goin on, I have still been hearing bad rumors about me & that kid Lance, my buddy. I dunno but *someone* definitely thinks we're like together and is saying that all over school. I think maybe it's Rick Wright again. He's still not over me. I don't understand what's goin on. I'll tell you what's goin on: *NOTHING!!*

BTW, I got this letter today in class from Emma. She wuz bored!

marybeth, 1/29

Hey babe what's up? I am so bored in math right now. I have 20 min. left and nothing to do so I am writing you this note. Lucky you! Last nite at SAT prep, that girl Gwen walked in (you know Gwen who we saw @ that party this year & who dissed Sherelle last summer—that Gwen) Anyway, she walked right into our room and Sherelle was sitting there right next to me and she made this mean ass face like she was saying get out. I was like settle down, Sher. Class sucked of course because all we really did was take a test for 3 hrs. I think maybe I'll come to your game today. I don't know. I wish Cliff could hang out too but I think his parents still won't allow him out. He said he will be, but I think he's just joking with me. He was saying that he needs to get his ass over to the mall because it's my birthday coming up. And then I smiled and told him I already had a valentine for him. He freaked on me (j/k of course) he was like oh why don't I just sign my paycheck over to you.

Do you think I will pass my driver's ed test? I cannot tell you how worried I am I have been worried like this all week long. Isn't that just crazy? I'm trying not to think about it. Wanna come to our hockey game tonight? Whatever if you do or don't. Have you talked to TJ lately? What's going

on with him? Oh well I am gonna stop
writing now because I think the bell is about
to ring. Talk to ya later! ♥ ya! Em

Emma cracks me up. Ouch my throat hurts. I hope
I am not sick that would suck. I'm so beat. Bed 4 me!

Teresa

Dear Diary,

I am sooooo excited! 2 months or something ago I
met this *really* cute guy at a hockey game, this guy Jesse.
He was nice enough. Anyway, last nite we hung out together. I saw him because he's friends w/Wendy's
boyfriend so we "double dated" I guess you could say.
We went to the movies. He's pretty cute or he was cute
last nite. The only problem is that he tries to go too far
when we're in the movie theater. I mean, I have morals,
right? Apparently he doesn't. So we did hook up and
had a good time. We just didn't go quite as far as I think
maybe he wanted to.

I was thinking today about the fact that I haven't seen
my brother in a very long time, we always come home at
different times and we end up not seeing each other. Even
though Vincent and I never ever talk about anything, I
still would like to know he's around. Is that weird of me to
think that and feel that way? I don't know anymore.

Onto a totally different subject: my work is *AWESOME*. I love it sooooo much. I got paid a lot for the last 2 weeks, which is totally good because I feel like I don't deserve that much. I would do this job for *FREE!* That's how much I love it.

Yeah, but I'm still glad it's the weekend!!

Billy

1-29

I cnt believe this has hapnd to me Rt now I am typing on the cmpter with only one arm. I fellyesterday in lacrose and fuckd up my sholdr soooooo bad. Im making so many spellin mistaks bc I am not used to typinhg with my lft hand and fingres 1 more things the doctr says I have a dislOcated shoulder cant play lacrosse for 3 wlks I am in a lot of pain now so I will say goodnight I m out

Kevin

1/29

hey hey hey it's sat. night. Nonono it's Fri, oh my bad. I can't believe like that's some serious shit that happened to Billy yesterday on the lacrosse field. Jake told me that Billy's shoulder like popped out of the socket which is gross i am soooo glad I wasn't there to see that today in school it wasn't too bad um I got like a D on some test but LOL I might be able to boost it to a C but who cares right now I don't remember what else happened cause it's late and I am kind of shit-faced right now um I went to a friend's party and since jonny can drive now he took me home so I love it he's the bomb no but really I am really drunk LOL I had a big ass screwdriver and beer. It was so freakin good not to have to worry tonite about drivin or not it was like a really freeing experience fm. how I have felt lately about the whole drinking & driving thing